THOMAS
AND THE EVANGELISTS

STUDIES IN BIBLICAL THEOLOGY

THOMAS
AND THE EVANGELISTS

H. E. W. TURNER

and

HUGH MONTEFIORE

SCM PRESS LTD
BLOOMSBURY STREET LONDON

FIRST PUBLISHED 1962
© SCM PRESS LTD 1962
PRINTED IN GREAT BRITAIN BY
W. & J. MACKAY & CO LTD, CHATHAM

CONTENTS

PREFACE

PART of the material contained in Canon Turner's contribution was delivered as a lecture during a visit to Codrington College, Barbados, in December 1959 and expanded into two Public Lectures in the Department of Theology in Durham in 1960.

Canon Montefiore's chapter in this book was originally published as an article in *New Testament Studies* Volume VII, 1961, pp. 220–48, and is reprinted here by kind permission of the Editor.

The Gospel of Thomas has already aroused considerable interest among students of the New Testament and patristic period. We believe that the importance of our subject is twofold. In the first place the Gospel of Thomas is a valuable fresh source document of early Christian gnosticism. So much of the Gospel of Thomas has some kind of relationship to the New Testament that the contrast between the beliefs and attitudes of the gnostic sects and those of the Great Church is seen here perhaps more clearly than in the more abstract gnostic treatises. The study of its spirituality may have more than a merely historical interest. In the second place the Gospel of Thomas presents us with problems of sources and origins that intimately concern the higher criticism of the canonical Gospels. Study of the Gospel of Thomas can illuminate the principles and methodology of gospel criticism, and it can force us to reconsider problems which may seem to have been settled by critical orthodoxy.

Neither of the contributors to this volume believe that these problems have yet been solved. Only a few years have passed since the text of the Gospel of Thomas was made available for critical study. Nevertheless it will be plain to the reader that the two contributors tend to return different answers to the difficult question of Thomas' direct dependence on the Synoptic Gospels. We place these essays before a wider circle of readers with the hope that the juxtaposition of our different viewpoints, together with the reasons why we hold them, may be of assistance to others in the resolution of this difficult problem.

H.E.W.T.
H.W.M.

ABBREVIATIONS

BJRL: *Bulletin of the John Rylands Library,* Manchester
CSCO: Corpus Scriptorum Christianorum Orientalium, Paris
CSEL: Corpus Scriptorum Ecclesiasticorum Latinorum, Vienna
Doresse: J. R. Doresse, *Les Paroles de Jésus,* Paris, 1959
ET: English translation
ExpT: *Expository Times,* Edinburgh
Gärtner: B. Gärtner, *The Theology of the Gospel of Thomas,* London,
1961
GCS: Die griechischen christlichen Schriftsteller der ersten drei
Jahrhunderte, Leipzig
Grant/Freedman: R. M. Grant and D. N. Freedman, *The Secret
Sayings of Jesus,* London, 1960
JTS: *Journal of Theological Studies,* Oxford
NT Apok.: *Neutestamentliche Apokryphen,* by E. Hennecke, 3rd
ed. rev. by W. Schneemelcher: Vol. I, The Gospels, Tübingen,
1959
NTS: *New Testament Studies,* London
PG: Migne, Patrologia Graeca, Paris
PL: Migne, Patrologia Latina, Paris
RevThPh: *Revue de Théologie et de Philosophie,* Geneva
TLZ: *Theologische Literaturzeitung,* Leipzig
TU: Texte und Untersuchungen zur Geschichte der altchrist-
lichen Literatur, Leipzig
VigChr: *Vigiliae Christianae,* Amsterdam
Wilson, *Studies:* R. McL. Wilson, *Studies in the Gospel of Thomas,*
London, 1960

I

THE GOSPEL OF THOMAS: ITS HISTORY, TRANSMISSION AND SOURCES

IN 1945 or 1946 (the circumstances of the discovery make a precise date impossible) thirteen MSS. written in Coptic were discovered at Nag Hammadi in Upper Egypt. They proved to be the remains of the library of a gnostic sect (probably Sethite), though some documents (notably the Gospel of Truth and other works in the Jung Codex) are plainly of Valentinian origin. Among the newly discovered works, one, a Gospel of Thomas purporting to contain Sayings of our Lord, is of outstanding interest not only to the theologian but also to a wider public.

The manuscript in which it is contained is variously numbered III (Puech) and X (Doresse). Judging by its size and appearance it formed the prize of the collection. It consists of some forty-two leaves folded so as to form 168 pages in a particularly fine script. Of these, twenty pages (ff. 80–99) are occupied by the Gospel of Thomas. The date assigned to the manuscript by scholars varies from the third to the fifth centuries, but perhaps a date around AD 400 is the most probable.[1]

Some at least of the works contained in this codex possessed special importance for this gnostic community. The first, the Apocryphon of John, is extant in three different editions in the collection, in each case placed first in the manuscript which contains it. Our Gospel is placed second, immediately followed by a Gospel of Philip which still awaits publication. The final work in the manuscript is entitled 'A Book of Thomas the Athlete, secret words spoken by the Saviour to Judas Thomas and preserved by Matthias'. The three apostles are familiar company in gnostic

---

[1] W. Till, 'New Sayings of Jesus in the recently discovered Coptic Gospel of Thomas', *BJRL* XLI, 1959, p. 451: *c.* 400; H. Puech in *NT Apok.*, p. 202: fourth to fifth centuries. The question partly depends upon the use of the cross in the form of an *ankh* (the Egyptian sign of life) which was not available before the destruction of the Serapeum in 391.

writings as the recipients of secret tradition, and Doresse makes the attractive suggestion that they represent the equivalent of Matthew, Mark and Luke of the Great Church.[1]

The place of origin of the Gospel of Thomas cannot be determined with any degree of certainty. Some indications favour Syria. In the Preamble Thomas is described as Didymus Judas Thomas, an expression paralleled in other Syrian documents such as the *Acts of Thomas*.[2] The tradition that Thomas was the twin brother of our Lord and was identical with the Judas of Mark 6.3 seems to have developed in Syria. However improbable this may be, it may serve to explain the appropriateness of Thomas as a recipient of secret revelation and even shed light on a cryptic passage in the Gospel of Thomas itself (Saying 13).[3] Quispel has called attention to a number of parallels with the Diatessaron of Tatian, which was widely current in Syria (and for some time the official text of the Gospels in the East Syrian Church), though he prefers the theory of common indebtedness to a third source, the Gospel of the Hebrews, to the hypothesis of direct relationship. Guillaumont even claims that Thomas was originally written in Syriac, though his arguments have not won general approval.[4]

At first sight an Egyptian origin for the Gospel might seem preferable. Our version is written in Coptic and there is an obviously close relationship to the Oxyrhynchus Sayings of Jesus. Some sayings certainly derive from the apocryphal Gospel of the Egyptians and its influence may have been even more extensive. Additional support might be forthcoming from the numerous parallels to Thomas in the Manichaean documents also preserved

---

[1] *Pistis Sophia* 42 f. (GCS, pp. 44 f.) describes them as the three witnesses. The suggestion is made by Doresse, p. 30. Puech, however (*NT Apok.*, p. 227), notes that the name of the redactor of the Book of Thomas the Athlete is given as Matthew, not Matthias.

[2] Doresse, p. 40. Parallels to five sayings in the Gospel from the *Acts of Thomas* (written in or near Edessa in the first half of the third century) are listed by Puech, *NT Apok.*, p. 207.

[3] The sayings are cited by the numbers in *The Gospel according to Thomas*, ed. and trans. by A. Guillaumont, H. C. Puech, G. Quispel, W. Till and Yassah 'abd Al Masîḥ, London and Leiden, 1959.

[4] A. Guillaumont, 'Semitismes dans les logia de Jesus retrouvés à Nag-Hammâdi', *Journal Asiatique CCXLVI*, 1958, pp. 113–23, criticized by Wilson, *Studies*, pp. 120–24.

in Coptic. But this evidence, while overwhelming in favour of Egypt as a centre of dissemination, cannot establish beyond doubt the place of origin.

Some vaguer indications of Western affinities are also forthcoming. Gärtner notes a number of parallels with Marcion, whose association with the gnostic Marcion dates from his visit to Rome. Both Marcion and Thomas display special indebtedness to Luke, though in very different ways. Tatian, no less than Marcion, worked at Rome, and F. C. Burkitt even maintained that the Diatessaron originated from Rome.[1] Valentinianism, a system whose documents contain many close parallels to Thomas, was also powerfully represented in the West.[2] Gärtner believes that the place of origin of the Gospel probably lay in the axis of gnostic influence which ran between Syria, Alexandria and Rome.[3] The evidence (though never conclusive) seems to be strongest at its Syrian end.[4]

At the risk of anticipating later discussion, something must be said here of the possible date of our document. External attestation of a Gospel of Thomas (usually without any indication of its contents) carries us back to the time of Hippolytus. In their present form the Oxyrhynchus Sayings of Jesus date from the end of the second century or the first quarter of the third, though their original editors were inclined to date their original compilation roughly to AD 140. Parallels to individual sayings are found as early as *II Clement* and St Irenaeus, though we have no means of knowing whether they are quoting the Gospel of Thomas or one of his sources. The use of the Gospel by Naassene and Valentinian Gnostics is probable, but does little to establish its date. While the compiler almost certainly used the apocryphal Gospels of the Hebrews and the Egyptians, this helps us little as their dates are equally unknown.[5] Gärtner, however, notes a fair measure of

---

[1] F. C. Burkitt, 'Tatian's Diatessaron and the Dutch Harmonies', *JTS* XXV, 1924, pp. 113–30; 'The Dura Fragment of Tatian', *JTS* XXXVI, 1935, pp. 255–9.

[2] Gärtner, pp. 26 f., 63–65, 66–68, 73 f., 150, 156 f., 175, 249 f.

[3] Gärtner, pp. 271 f.

[4] This view is supported by W. C. van Unnik, *Newly Discovered Gnostic Writings*, ET (SBT 30), 1960, p. 49; L. Cerfaux, 'Les Parables du Royaume', *Muséon* LXX, 1957, p. 319; Guillaumont, *art. cit.,* p. 117; Puech, *NT Apok.,* p. 207; Doresse, pp. 73 f.

[5] Wilson, *Studies*, pp. 7 f.

agreement on a date between AD 140 and 150, though perhaps a decade or two later might not be altogether excluded.[1]

A Gospel of Thomas 'the Israelite philosopher', preserved partly in Greek and partly in Latin, was known before the recent discoveries.[2] It is devoted to infancy narratives and is one of a series of works (not necessarily of heretical intention) designed to 'supplement' the scanty data given in the Gospels. Its historical value cannot be rated highly and the presentation of our Lord falls well below synoptic standards. One incident in this Gospel depicts Jesus as teaching his schoolmaster the deeper significance of the letters of the alphabet. St Irenaeus (who clearly believed that the story had a heretical and probably a Marcosian origin) records a slightly different version.[3] There is a possible parallel in Saying 4 of the present collection in a saying quoted expressly from Thomas by Hippolytus.[4] A third form of the saying recurs in a Manichaean Psalm-book.[5] It looks as if we are concerned here with material preserved both in narrative and saying form and somewhat malleable in character. There is no further point of contact between the two documents and even this may be accidental.

Allusions to a Gospel of Thomas (without further indication of its content) are found in Eusebius, St Jerome and St Ambrose.[6] In two passages St Cyril of Jerusalem warns his catechumens against a Gospel of Thomas which he believes to be of Manichaean origin.[7] If this is to be identified with our present Gospel, the date implied would be too late, but the parallels in Manichaean documents noted by Doresse indicate a wide currency in these

[1] Gärtner, p. 271.
[2] O. Cullmann in *NT Apok.*, pp. 293–99; ET in M. R. James, *Apocryphal New Testament*, 1924, pp. 49–65.
[3] Irenaeus, *Adv. haer.* 1.13.1 (Harvey I, pp. 177 f.).
[4] Hippolytus, *Ref.* 5.7.21. On the relation between this passage and Saying 4 see Wilson, *Studies*, pp. 33 f.; Puech, *NT Apok.*, pp. 203 f.
[5] *Manichaean Psalm-Book*, ed. C. R. C. Allberry, 1938, p. 192, cited by Doresse, p. 128.
[6] Eusebius, *Hist. eccl.* 3.25.6; Jerome, *Comm. in Matt.* Prol. (PL 26.17A); Ambrose, *Exp. in Luc.* 1.2 (CSEL 32.4, pp. 10 f.), probably dependent upon Origen (cited below).
[7] Cyril of Jerusalem, *Orat. Catech.* 4.36; 6.31 (PG 33. 500B, 593A). Writers dependent on Cyril are listed by Puech, *NT Apok.*, p. 200. The description of Cyril's evidence by Wilson, *Studies*, p. 11, is somewhat misleading.

circles at least in Egypt.[1] It is certainly possible that some gnostics attached themselves to Manicheism after the collapse of their movement.

More significant clues are provided by Hippolytus and Origen. As we have already seen, Hippolytus links the name of Thomas to a form of Saying 4 current among the Naassenes. This is notably divergent from the text of our Gospel both in Greek and Coptic. Puech suggests that at this point the Naassenes may have altered their text of Thomas or quoted it with considerable freedom. But the analogy of the various editions of the Apocryphon of John leaves room for the conjecture that different versions of the same fundamental document may have been current within gnosticism.[2] A considerably closer parallel to Saying 11 (without further indication of its source) occurs in the same document.[3] Origen alludes to a Gospel of Thomas in general terms in his comments on the opening words of Luke and quotes Saying 82 elsewhere without disclosing his source.[4] Both writers, however, mention a document of this name and reveal some knowledge of one saying which forms part of its contents.

Parallels to particular sayings are by no means infrequent both in orthodox and heretical writings. Puech makes a conservative count of eighteen passages.[5] Orthodox writers include St Augustine (Saying 52 'from some heretical writing or other'), Lactantius (Saying 19), Ephraem Syrus (Saying 30), the Syrian *Didascalia* (Saying 48), St Irenaeus (Saying 19), and *II Clement* (Saying 22).[6] But by far the largest contributor is Clement of Alexandria with six quotations or near parallels.[7] It is to be noticed

---

[1] Cf. Sayings 4, 5, 7, 17, 19, 30, 37, 38, 55, 60, 76, 90, 94, 108 in Doresse's commentary *ad loc.*

[2] Hipp. *Ref.* 5.7.21; Saying 4, set out in tabular form with brief discussion in Grant/Freedman, pp. 80 f.; Puech, *NT Apok.*, pp. 203 f.

[3] Hipp. *Ref.* 5.8.32.

[4] Origen, *Hom. in Luc.* I (GCS IX, p. 5); *Hom. in Jer.* XX.3 (PG 13. 531D f.); cf. Didymus, *Comm. in Ps.* 88.8 (PG 39.1488D).

[5] Puech, *NT Apok.*, pp. 216–19.

[6] Augustine, *C. advers. legis et prophetarum* 2.4, 14 (PL 42. 647); Lactantius, *Div. inst.* 4.8 (CSEL 19, p. 295); Ephraem Syrus, *Ev. concord. exp.* 14.24 (CSCO 137, p. 144); Syrian *Didascalia* 15 (Connolly, p. 134; cf. TU 25.2, p. 345); Irenaeus, *Dem. Ev. Apost.* 43; *II Clem.* 12.2–6.

[7] Clement of Alexandria, *Strom.* 2.9, § 45.5, and 5.14, § 96.3: Saying 2; 3.13, § 92.2: Saying 22; 3.15, § 99.4, cf. *Ecl. proph.* 14.1: Saying 27; 3.13, § 92.2: Saying 37. Parallels to Salome, the interlocutor in Saying 61, occur

that writers of a Syrian or Egyptian origin predominate. In most cases there is no evidence one way or the other as to the source of their information. St Augustine has either forgotten or prefers not to mention the document which he is quoting. The balance of probability favours the view that both Hippolytus (or his source) and Origen knew our document. Some of the parallels in Clement (and possibly all) are drawn from sources of Thomas rather than from the Gospel itself. Thus so far as orthodox writers are concerned there is no reliable external evidence for the existence of the Gospel before the time of Hippolytus and Origen or the first quarter of the third century. Parallels to the Gospel of Thomas from gnostic sources will be examined later.

So far we have been concerned with the date and place of origin of the Gospel of Thomas, its external attestation as a document and the parallels to individual sayings contained in orthodox writers. We must now make some attempt to trace its history and possible sources. Much no doubt will continue to remain obscure and scholarly discussion has barely begun. Fresh light on the problem will no doubt be shed by other documents from Nag Hammadi, though, as the field of discussion widens, new problems are certain to present themselves. Many of the suggestions made here must be regarded as provisional in the highest degree. It will become apparent that the conclusions reached by Canon Montefiore are not in some important respects identical with my own. There is only to be expected in the present state of the question.

It is pleasant to begin with a famous question which has been solved by the discovery of our document.[1] It is the source of the Sayings of Jesus (preserved in Greek) discovered by Grenfell and Hunt at Oxyrhynchus in Middle Egypt in 1897 and 1903. That this rich and miscellaneous collection contained gnostic writings has now been confirmed by the identification by Puech of another fragment (Pap.Oxy.1081) as part of the Greek text of another gnostic writing, the *Sophia Jesu Christi*, preserved in

in four further passages. It cannot, however, be assumed that these are necessarily taken from the Gospel of Thomas. Some of the passages mention the Gospel of the Egyptians as their source.

[1] This identification was first made independently by Puech and Garitte, but the priority belongs to Puech (see *NT Apok.*, p. 61 n. 1).

Coptic in a Berlin manuscript 8502 and included in the Nag Hammadi collection, but not yet edited.[1]

The Sayings of Jesus form three complexes classified as Pap. Oxy.1, 654 and 655 respectively. They derive from three manuscripts dated by the editors from the end of the second century or the beginning of the third.[2] Scribal errors indicate that they were copied from an earlier document and the editors were perhaps prophetic in conjecturing that the original compilation was made 'not later than AD 140'.[3]

It now appears that the Oxyrhynchus Sayings formed part of a Greek version of the Gospel of Thomas. Thus Pap. Oxy. 654 contains the Preamble to the Gospel and the first seven sayings torn down the middle, while Pap. Oxy. 1 covers Sayings 26–33, together with Saying 77, which the Coptic text separates from Saying 30 and combines with different material to form a new unit. Pap. Oxy. 655 comprises Sayings 36–39 in the Coptic version.[4]

Scholars are agreed that the Greek version represents an earlier form of what is fundamentally the same tradition as the Coptic. Whether this is sufficient to establish the view that the Gospel of Thomas was originally written in Greek is more open to doubt. Guillaumont favours Syriac as the language of origin and Garitte, while not necessarily disputing the possibility of a Greek original, regards the Greek version as secondary to the Coptic version.[5] At present, however, the balance of argument favours the hypothesis of a Greek original.

Comparison of the full text of the Gospel with the Oxyrhynchus fragments strongly suggests that the Coptic is more than a translation; it represents an edition. Thus, despite the deplorable condition of its preservation, the Greek Preamble merely mentions

---

[1] Puech, *op. cit.*, pp. 169 f.

[2] Pap. Oxy. 1 'not much later than AD 200'; Pap. Oxy. 654 'middle or end of the third century; a later date than AD 300 is most unlikely'; Pap. Oxy. 655 'not likely to have been much later than AD 250' (Grenfell and Hunt, quoted by Wilson, *Studies*, p. 7 n. 1).

[3] W. Schneemelcher, *NT Apok.*, pp. 61 f.; Wilson, *Studies*, p. 146.

[4] Tables in Puech, *NT Apok.*, p. 213; Wilson, *Studies*, pp. 157 f. Schneemelcher, *NT Apok.*, pp. 61–72, sets out both versions in German translation with brief discussion.

[5] Guillaumont, *art. cit.*; G. Garitte, 'Les "Logoi" d'Oxyrhynque et l'apocryphe copte dit "Evangile de Thomas" ', *Muséon* LXXIII, 1960, pp. 151–73.

Thomas and leaves no room for the fuller description of the Apostle in the Coptic text. The first saying ends with the words 'and he will reign' (i.e. be a king), whereas the Coptic adds the gnosticizing touch 'over the All'. The most familiar of the Oxyrhynchus Sayings reads as follows: 'Where there are two, they are not without God; and where there is one alone, I say I am with him. Lift the stone and there thou shalt find me; cleave the wood, and I am there.' This forms a smooth and natural unity which is disturbed in the Coptic by the dislocation of the Saying and the introduction of echoes which seem to be secondary. Saying 30 reads: 'Where there are three gods, there are gods, where there are two or one, there am I with them.' The introduction of the number three may possibly be an allusion to the three natures or races of mankind under their celestial patrons or (less probably) a Trinitarian echo intruded into the saying and somewhat out of harmony with the document as a whole. The second half of the Greek logion is combined with a saying about Light and the All, both well-known gnostic themes, to form Saying 77. The new connexion is by no means obvious, but my friend, Dr K. H. Kuhn, has recently made the attractive suggestion that it may depend upon a play upon words available only in Coptic between 'attain to' and 'cleave'.[1] Finally, if Puech is right in reconstructing the end of Saying 5 in the Greek version by means of a grave wrapping also found at Oxyrhynchus, the Coptic editor has omitted a reference to the resurrection of the dead.

Gärtner, on the other hand, while not denying the possibility of tendentious editing, prefers the view that the alterations are due to faulty transmission and incompetent translation. He calls attention to the fact that the Greek version is longer than the Coptic, although we might expect a tendentious revision to have the opposite effect. Yet in one notable case (Saying 36) where the Greek form is probably a conflate of Matt. 6.25 and 28 and Luke 12.22 and 27 the shorter Coptic version is better explained as a contraction in order to emphasize the editor's conscientious abhorrence of the body. This explanation is certainly supported by the content of the succeeding saying, which has a similar theme. While the possibilities noted by Gärtner may have contributed to the

[1] K. H. Kuhn, 'Some observations in the Coptic Gospel according to Thomas', *Muséon* LXXIII, 1960, pp. 317 f.

situation, the theory of tendentious editing covers more of the facts and remains more convincing.[1]

The extent of the Coptic redaction must not, however, be exaggerated. Not only does the Gospel of Thomas in its present form retain elements drawn from non-gnostic sources which have not been too obviously assimilated to their new setting, but even the Greek version is not wholly free from gnostic or gnosticizing features.[2] The judgment of Kasser, that if the Coptic contains enough biblical elements to be described as a Christian apocryphon rather than as a gnostic document, the Greek bears very clearly the marks of gnosis, may well contain a measure of exaggeration in both halves of the statement; he is certainly not in error in reducing the difference between them to one of degree rather than of kind.[3]

The gnostic affinities of the Gospel of Thomas may therefore be regarded as beyond question. This is supported by other converging lines of testimony. Parallels to individual sayings of varying degrees of closeness occur in gnostic documents or are attributed to gnostic schools in other sources. Three sayings are echoed in the *Pistis Sophia*, a Barbelo-gnostic work dating from about the middle of the third century.[4] Here Salome, mentioned in Saying 61, is a frequent interlocutor. The Naassene document preserved by Hippolytus contains an almost exact quotation of Saying 11 as well as what is perhaps a portmanteau allusion to Sayings 2–4. From the closely related Ophite group comes a quotation of Saying 74 recorded by Celsus in his anti-Christian work, the *Alethes Logos*, written about AD 178. [5] Saying 23 is cited fron a Basilidean source.[6] Valentinian documents appear to display knowledge of Saying 114.[7] At least one logion (Saying 38) and possibly another (Saying 4) was current among the Marcosians.[8] Not all these

[1] Gärtner, pp. 82–87.

[2] Doresse, p. 69.

[3] R. Kasser, 'Les manuscrits de Nag-Hammâdi: faits, documents, problèmes', *RevThPh* 1959, p. 364. I owe this reference to Wilson, *Studies*, p. 68.

[4] *Pistis Sophia* 100 (p. 161), 102 (p. 164): Saying 2; 134 (p. 229): Saying 23; 134 (p. 228): Saying 91.

[5] Origen, *C. Cels.* 8.15 f. (GCS II, pp. 232 f.).

[6] Iren., *Adv. haer.* 1.19.3 (I, p. 202); Epiphanius, *Haer.* 24.5.

[7] Clement, *Exc. Theod.* 21.3, and Heracleon in Origen, *Comm. in Jo.* 6.20, § 111 (GCS IV, p. 129): Saying 114.

[8] Iren., *Adv. haer.* 1.13.2 (I, p. 179): Saying 38; 1.13.1 (I, pp. 177 f.): Saying 4 (?).

parallels are equally conclusive. Some, for example, may depend upon the sources of Thomas rather than upon the Gospel itself, or represent different forms of floating material, but dependence upon our document is probable both for the Naassene and Valentinian evidence. This would carry the date of the Gospel of Thomas back into the second century, but our knowledge of the rise and evolution of the gnostic movement does not extend to precise chronology.

Important indications of the theological climate of Thomas are provided by parallels in the gnostic documents. Gärtner regards Valentinian sources as of particular importance. As early as 1911 Carola Barth published a detailed study of Valentinian exegesis, and the field of comparison has been greatly extended in the intervening period.[1] The use of Lucan material in the Gospel of Thomas, to which Gärtner calls attention, is noted by St Irenaeus as a special feature of Valentinianism.[2] The same Father also criticizes the Valentinian tendency to conflate and alter the order of canonical material.[3] The appeal to the parables of Jesus represents an additional common feature.[4] Decisive importance in determining the circles in which our document was compiled is attached by Gärtner to the Gospel of Truth, a Valentinian homily discovered at Nag Hammadi. 'If the Gospel of Truth is reckoned as coming from Valentinian circles, the same ought to apply to the Gospel of Thomas, since the resemblance between the two is so great.'[5] If there is reason to suspect an element of exaggeration in this judgment, the Gospel of Truth certainly clarifies a number of mysterious terms and ideas in Thomas. 'Totality' in this document obviously bears a close resemblance to 'the All' in our Gospel. The Parable of the Lost Sheep occurs in both, and a possible application of the Parable of the Woman with the Leaky Jar in Thomas may be found in the Gospel of Truth.[6] Other parallels

[1] C. Barth, *Die Interpretation des Neuen Testaments in der valentinianischen Gnosis* (TU 38.3, pp. 1–118).

[2] Iren., *Adv. haer.* 3.14.3 (II, p. 78); cf. Origen, *Hom. in Luc.* XVI (IX, p. 108); Gärtner, pp. 66–68.

[3] Iren., *Adv. haer.* 1.1.15 (I, pp. 66–68).

[4] Barth, *op. cit.*, pp. 59–65.

[5] Gärtner, p. 272.

[6] Gospel of Truth 31.36–32.18 (Grobel's ed., 1960, pp. 128–34) with a highly individual exegesis: Saying 107; Gospel of Truth 25.25–30 (p. 102) and 26.10–15 (p. 104): Saying 97.

are to be found in the *Excerpta e Theodoto* contained in the writings of Clement of Alexandria. There is an allusion to the Parable of the Mustard Seed.[1] The mysterious lion symbol used in the Gospel of Thomas is found in the *Excerpts* combined with a reference to the world.[2] The contrast between image and likeness is here made the basis for the distinction between the three natures of mankind.[3] The male/female differentiation which represents a familiar theme in Thomas also occurs in this document.[4] An attractive conjecture on the use and even the original purpose of our Gospel based on the concluding section of the *Letter of Ptolemaeus to Flora* would point in the same direction.[5]

But Valentinianism is not the only gnostic system to contain parallels to the Gospel of Thomas. Professor R. M. Grant has made out an attractive case for a close relationship between the Naassenes and our document.[6] Parables used in common include the Sower, the Mustard Seed, the Leaven, and the Hid Treasure.[7] In both the concept of the Kingdom (following Luke 17.20–22) is strongly interiorized.[8] James the Just and Mariamme occur in both documents.[9] Of greater importance may be parallels to the distinctive material in Thomas. The three words of power of the Naassenes may serve to explain the three words addressed by our Lord to Thomas in Saying 13.[10] In a document probably intended for a wider public than the gnostic initiates the reference could not be made more explicit. Other common features include the image of the corpse and the notion of spiritual man as androgynous.[11] Both use the simile of stripping garments.[12] An even

[1] *Exc. Theod.* 1.3: Saying 20.
[2] *Exc. Theod.* 84: Saying 7.
[3] *Exc. Theod.* 50: Sayings 22, 83 f.
[4] *Exc. Theod.* 21.2 f.: Sayings 22, 114.
[5] R. M. Grant, 'Notes on the Gospel of Thomas', *VigChr* XIII, 1959, p. 173; Wilson, *Studies*, p. 13.
[6] Grant, *art. cit.*, pp. 173–9; cf. Grant/Freedman, esp. pp. 80–84 and 92–96.
[7] The Sower, Hipp. *Ref.* 5.8.29 f. and Saying 9; the Mustard Seed, *Ref.* 5.9.6. and Saying 20; the Leaven, *Ref.* 5.8.8 and Saying 96; the Hid Treasure, *Ref.* 5.8.8 and Saying 109.
[8] *Ref.* 5.7.20 f. and Sayings 2 and 113.
[9] *Ref.* 5.7.1 and Sayings 12, 21 and 114.
[10] *Ref.* 5.8.4 and Saying 13.
[11] The corpse, *Ref.* 5.8.22 and Sayings 56 and 60; androgyny, *Ref.* 5.7.14 and Sayings 22 and 114.
[12] *Ref.* 5.8.44 and Saying 37.

more striking feature is the conflation of canonical material of which Grant gives a number of examples from the Naassene document.

This is an impressive accumulation of parallels, especially when it is recalled that Naassene material is not as plentiful as the Valentinian documents. More parables are laid under contribution in the Naassene than in the Valentinian documents. If St Irenaeus regards conflation as a Valentinian speciality, examples in the extant documents of this school are relatively few, whereas Naassene parallels are significantly close. The documents of both schools contain affinities to the material distinctive to Thomas. Here the Naassene sources are a least as significant as the Valentinian.

The evidence for the use of the Gospel of Thomas and the material which it contains in gnostic circles is overwhelmingly strong. It is, however, difficult to feel as confident as both Gärtner and Grant appear to be that their particular source was the one in which the Gospel originated. Many of the features to which they call attention are not confined to one particular sect. The preservation of gnostic documents has been attended by too many elements of chance to make a confident judgment really admissible. If the recent discoveries place the study of gnosticism on a much more secure foundation, we are not yet in a position to determine either the precise opinions or even the comparative influence of particular schools of thought within the movement as a whole. Both cases are admittedly strong, but to an uncomfortable extent appear to cancel each other out. Whether the Gospel of Thomas was originally compiled in some part of the gnostic movement incapable at present of more exact identification is still open to debate. Puech conjectures that the Thomas tradition existed in at least two editions, the one earlier and more orthodox, the other used in gnostic and Manichaean circles.[1] His argument has not as yet been fully presented, but appears to rest upon the fact that the Greek version is notably less gnostic than the Coptic edition. His completion of Saying 5 from a grave wrapping discovered at Oxyrhynchus might tend in the same direction. But the differences between the Greek and the Coptic can easily be exaggerated and are probably only matters of degree. The more orthodox features in the Gospel may either be unelided

[1] Puech, *NT Apok.*, pp. 221 f.

elements in the sources or features in the orthodox tradition assimilated to gnosticism by processes with which we are not at present familiar. The absorptive capacity of gnosticism must not be set too low, especially in the circumstances of the second century, when gnosticism and orthodoxy existed side by side and a sharp competition for souls can safely be inferred from the documents on both sides. The counter-hypothesis that Thomas was compiled within the gnostic movement from earlier and more orthodox sources remains at least a strong possibility.

The Gospel itself bears clear traces of dependence upon earlier sources. Parallels to individual sayings are attributed to apocryphal Gospels by orthodox writers. Thus a close approximation to Saying 2 is attributed by Clement of Alexandria to the Gospel of the Hebrews.[1] The Gospel of the Nazarenes (which may be another version of the Gospel of the Hebrews) contains a parallel to the opening sentence of Saying 104.[2] A possible (though far from certain) parallel to Saying 99 is contained in a fragment from the Gospel of the Ebionites.[3] Explicit quotation of the known fragments of the Gospel of the Egyptians does not seem to occur, but a number of probable echoes exist. It is perhaps worth recalling the role assigned to the Gospels of the Hebrews and the Egyptians in earlier discussions of the Oxyrhynchus Logia.[4] While they are demonstrably wrong so far as the origin of the document is concerned they may provide some indication of the probable source of certain sayings.

The sources of the Gospel of Thomas cannot be determined with any degree of certainty. The method of its construction does not favour any easy breakdown into sources. Small runs of material certainly occur, but a more normal (though by no means universal) procedure seems to have been the connexion of material by means of catchword or similarity of theme. Yet the contents of the Gospel do not possess the same theological texture throughout. In one run of Sayings (73–75) we can almost watch a common

[1] Clem. *Strom.* 5.14, § 96.3.
[2] Jerome, *Adv. Pelag.* 3.2 (PL 23. 597 f.); *Comm. in Isa.* 11.2 (PL 24.148).
[3] Epiph. *Haer.* 30.14.5; see G. Quispel, 'The Gospel of Thomas and the New Testament', *VigChr* XI, 1957, p. 191; but cf. J. B. Bauer in W. C. van Unnik, *Evangelien aus dem Nilsand*, 1960 (expanded German ed. of *Newly Discovered Gnostic Writings*), p. 120.
[4] Puech, *NT Apok.*, p. 214.

theme in the process of evolution. Saying 73 represents a good tradition; Saying 74 is almost certainly apocryphal; while the evidence of Celsus confirms the impression that Saying 75 is purely gnostic. Doublets of individual sayings occur, often widely separated in the Gospel itself, and it would be a natural conjecture in these cases to infer a difference of source. Quispel notes four instances, Sayings 51 (though Saying 3 is perhaps a more natural parallel) and 113, 48 and 106, 55 and 101, 89 and 22.[1] Less obvious and perhaps more questionable are Sayings 41 and 70.[2] Possibly Sayings 12 and 13, which give positions of prominence to James the Just and Thomas himself, might also be included in the list. Quispel conjectures that his pairs belong to the Gospels of the Hebrews and of the Egyptians respectively, but in any case his further point, that this suggests that the more gnostic stream in the Gospel depends upon a less heterodox form of what is virtually a single tradition, seems true and important. It is by no means certain that this more orthodox strand in the Gospel of Thomas is not, in fact, the canonical tradition, while some seem to go beyond anything that can be colourably attributed to the Gospel of the Egyptians.

A Jewish-Christian source behind the Gospel of Thomas seems wholly probable. Gnosticism was hospitable to many influences, Judaism and Jewish Christianity included. The evolution of Jewish Christianity has attracted much attention of late, thanks to the researches of Schoeps, Strecker, Daniélou and others.[3] Its influence upon gnosticism is carefully studied in Wilson's fine book, *The Gnostic Problem*.[4] If there is some reason to doubt whether all the material derived by Daniélou from this source is really Jewish-Christian in origin, the older account of a dwindling and insignificant movement can no longer be maintained.[5]

Quispel has paid particular attention to this source in a series of

---

[1] G. Quispel, 'Some Remarks on the Gospel of Thomas', *NTS* V, 1959, pp. 287 f.; *VigChr* XI, p. 200.

[2] Grant/Freedman, pp. 147 and 164.

[3] H. J. Schoeps, *Urgemeinde, Judenchristentum, Gnosis*, 1956; G. Strecker, *Das Judenchristentum in der Pseudoclementinen* (TU 70), 1958; J. Daniélou, *Théologie du Judéo-christianisme*, 1958.

[4] Published in 1958.

[5] The views of Daniélou are criticized by J. Munck in 'Jewish Christianity in Post-apostolic Times', *NTS* VI, 1960, pp. 103–16.

important articles.[1] He attempts to frame objective criteria for identifying the material in Thomas which comes from this milieu. The presence of Aramaisms is valuable evidence which can be employed to good effect even when a saying approximates most closely to the canonical tradition. Jewish or Jewish-Christian concepts or parallels in literature with known Jewish-Christian tendencies such as the Pseudo-Clementine *Homilies* and *Recognitions* is a further important criterion. Finally (and most extensively used by Quispel) the presence of variants in common with the Diatessaron of Tatian is of considerable significance for his argument.

Before proceeding to an evaluation of these criteria we must develop his argument on the third criterion somewhat more fully. Here Quispel is recalling a theory of which his articles sketch the previous history and applying it with considerable skill to the Gospel of Thomas. A tradition preserved by Victor of Capua (and possibly supported by a passage in Epiphanius) described the Diatessaron (the Fourfold Harmony) as a Diapente or Fivefold Harmony.[2] He follows Baumstark in identifying this source with the Apocryphal Gospel of the Hebrews. The Stichometry of Nicephorus Callistus assigns to this document a length of 2,200 lines. For purposes of comparison the same author estimates Matthew as 2,500 lines and a Gospel of Thomas (possibly though not certainly to be identified with our document) as 1,300.[3] While, as we have seen, relatively few of the extant fragments of this and closely related Gospels have clear parallels in Thomas, Quispel regards it as probable that it is the source of something like half the sayings in our document.

This is certainly an economical and far-reaching hypothesis with considerable weight of evidence in its support. It cannot,

---

[1] G. Quispel, *NTS* V, 1959, pp. 276–90, and *VigChr* XI, 1957, pp. 189–207; 'L'évangile selon Thomas et les Clementines', *VigChr* XII, 1958, pp. 181–96; 'L'évangile selon Thomas et le Diatessaron', *VigChr* XIII, 1959, pp. 87–117. According to Quispel, roughly half the sayings in our document come from this source. He has not committed himself to a definitive list. The following sayings are discussed in his articles in this connexion: 2, 6, 8 f., 12, 16, 21, 25, 32 f., 35 f., 39 f., 44 f., 47 f., 54 f., 57 f., 62 (?), 63–66, 68, 76, 78, 86, 89–91, 93–100, 102, 104, 109, 113.

[2] Victor of Capua, *Praef. in evang. harm.* 1 (PL 68, 253); cf. Epiph. *Haer.* 46.1.9.

[3] Nicephorus Callistus, *Chron.* (PG 100. 1060), quoted by Vielhauer in *NT Apok.*, p. 88.

however, be considered at present as more than a working hypothesis and there are strong arguments on the other side. The origin and reliability of the tradition recorded by Victor of Capua are shrouded in obscurity, and it may be little more than a personal conjecture, or a misunderstanding of Epiphanius. The Italian Jesuit Messina in his edition of the Persian Diatessaron pointed out that the extra-canonical sources of the Diatessaron cannot be confined to the Gospel of the Hebrews. An apocryphal Infancy Gospel, the *Protevangelium of James*, now only preserved in Syriac but probably translated from a Greek original, was certainly laid under contribution.[1] Quispel dismisses this argument as of secondary importance, but it may have greater significance than he allows.[2] The so-called Aramaisms may not be satisfactory evidence for an early Aramaic Gospel tradition transmitted through the Gospel of the Hebrews independently of the Synoptics. Some may be general Semitisms reminiscent of the possible Syrian origin of our Gospel even if the more extensive theory of Guillaumont is unlikely to prove acceptable in its present form. Certainly, as Dr Kuhn reminds us, the influence of Coptic upon the transmission of the tradition would repay further specialist investigation.[3] The recent work of Strecker on the Pseudo-Clementines casts doubt on the theory that a Jewish Christian Gospel is being laid under contribution. Quispel's parallels from this source are drawn indifferently from the *Homilies* and the *Recognitions* and from both the Latin and Syriac versions. Questions of textual transmission and *Quellenkritik* are involved here to which at present no decisive answer can be returned.[4] Gärtner also points out that variants found in Thomas are not merely paralleled in the Diatessaron and the Pseudo-Clementines. The field of comparison must be widened to include the Western Text and even Justin Martyr. The inference might be that instead of a straight line going back to an early Aramaic tradition we should think rather of a more widely diffused textual tradition dating from the middle of the second century or slightly earlier.[5] In his

[1] G. Messina, *Diatessaron Persiano*, Rome, 1943, pp. lii–lix.
[2] Quispel, *VigChr* XIII, 1959, p. 109.
[3] K. H. Kuhn, *Muséon* LXXIII, 1960, pp. 317–23.
[4] Wilson, *Studies*, pp. 127–32; Gärtner, pp. 62–65; Grant, *VigChr* XIII, 1959, p. 174.
[5] Gärtner, pp. 63–65.

discussion of particular sayings Wilson shows that alternative
explanations are admissible in a large number of cases. Some
of the traces of the Aramaic tradition are obviously secondary. A
completed parallelism may be a pedantic expansion in the course
of tradition. Some of the variants common to Thomas and the
Diatessaron may not be significant. In other cases gnostic
editorial activity may be a more natural explanation. Identical
editorial revision ought possibly to be taken into account.
Wilson's list of possible cases is decidedly shorter than that of
Quispel.[1] Much patient work by scholars will need to be done
before we are in a position to assess the validity of Quispel's
hypothesis, but the warning that his full-scale integration of the
evidence may not be conclusive is certainly salutary even at this
stage of discussion. As we attempt to probe behind material
probably dating from the middle of the second century to
a tradition parallel to but independent of the canonical
Gospels, it is easy to get caught in a tangled web of unproven
hypotheses.

Whatever may come to be thought about Quispel's wide-
ranging theory, there are strong indications that Thomas was
indebted to the Gospel of the Hebrews, though the extent of this
indebtedness cannot be determined on grounds of content alone.
Thus the attribution of Saying 2 to this source is attested by
Clement of Alexandria, though it would have been difficult to
infer this conclusion from the logion itself. The argument from
doublets may be of some weight, and one or two probable sayings
from this source may be gleaned by this method. The Gospel of
the Hebrews is probably the source of Saying 12, which reads as
follows: 'The disciples said to Jesus: We know that thou wilt go
away from us. Who is it who shall be great over us? Jesus said
to them: Wherever you have come, you will go to James the
righteous for whose sake heaven and earth came into being.' Here
the place to which they will go is clearly earthly rather than
heavenly or inward as is normal in Thomas. The exaltation of
James (correctly described as the Just) is characteristic of Jewish
Christianity, though it also occurs in gnostic (Naassene) sources.
Grant notes that if the form of the saying is Jewish or Jewish-
Christian, its intention is precisely the opposite, but this is a

[1] Wilson, *Studies*, pp. 117–41.

matter not of source but of application.[1] Jewish legend knew of others for whose sakes heaven and earth were created. A difference of source is indicated by the next saying, which assigns an even more splendid position to Thomas himself. The impression may be left upon the reader that in this saying we have a Jewish-Christian counterblast to the Petrine passage in Matt. 16.17–19.[2] A second passage (Saying 104) finds a parallel in the Gospel of the Nazarenes: 'They said to him: come let us pray today and let us fast. Jesus said: Which then is the sin that I have committed, or in what have I been vanquished? But when the bridegroom comes out of the bridal chamber, then let them fast and let them pray.' The passage in the source is obviously an extension of Matt. 3.13–15, though the point is obscured in the Gospel of Thomas, which has no incident to which it could be attached. The second half recalls Mark 2.18–20, but makes a further point about prayer which is in line with a long-standing Jewish usage which forbids the practice of prayer on the wedding night. The Greek form of Saying 30 (significantly altered in the Coptic version) seems to have a similar source. 'Where there are two, they are not without God.' The obvious Gospel parallel is Matt. 18.20, but there is a clear parallel to both in *Pirke Aboth*. More subject to debate is a group of two sayings (27 and 53) which refer to Jewish instititutions such as fasting, the sabbath and circumcision. The former speaks of fasting to the world and keeping the sabbath as sabbath. Both expressions are paralleled in the writings of the Fathers.[3] A gnostic application of the saying is easy to find. If the topics to which it alludes are clearly of interest to Jewish Christians, its provenance is by no means certain. The latter saying deals with circumcision in a highly distinctive way to which I have been unable to find any parallel in the Fathers. His disciples ask Jesus whether circumcision is profitable or not. 'He said to them: If it were profitable, their father would beget them circumcised from their mother. But the true circumcision of the Spirit has become

---

[1] Grant, *VigChr* XIII, 1959, p. 172.

[2] That gnosticism could lay claim to great Christian figures from other traditions is proved by Clement, *Strom.* 7.17, § 106.4, where it is stated that the Basilideans and Valentinians tried to incorporate the pillar apostles of the Great Church (Peter and Paul) into their systems.

[3] Fasting to the world: Clement, *Strom.* 3.15, § 99.4; *Ecl. proph.* 14.1. Sabbatize the sabbath: Justin, *Dial.* 12.3; Tertullian, *Adv. Jud.* 4 (PL 2. 605).

profitable in every way.' Pauline parallels are obvious and clear; indeed the word 'profitable' is a direct transliteration from St Paul's Greek.[1] But the Pauline argument never loses sight of the real significance of circumcision as a mark of the covenant. A Jewish-Christian source is here unlikely, not least because of the clear indebtedness to St Paul. Even more tentatively we may examine a cryptic passage which immediately follows Saying 104, which can with fair confidence be ascribed to a Jewish-Christian source. 'Jesus said: Whoever knows father and mother shall be called the son of a harlot.' It might even be preferable (following Doresse) to read a question mark. The reference is probably to Jesus and the concluding words probably pick up the implied slur on our Lord's human birth in John 8.41. It is unfortunately true that this is repeated several times in the Talmud. The allusion may well be to his divine sonship and his human birth of the Virgin Mary. This is certainly not the Christology of Thomas, but it is not likely to be that of the Gospel to the Hebrews either. But another interpretation is possible which would bring the saying wholly into line with a particularly well-documented fragment of the Gospel of the Hebrews.[2] On this view while God would still be the Father, the mother would be the Holy Spirit. But the interpretation of the saying is too uncertain to admit of any secure inference.

An even stronger case can be made out for a close connexion between the Gospel of Thomas and the Gospel of the Egyptians, even on the basis of the few fragments of the latter which we possess. Quispel makes a somewhat far-reaching claim that the more syncretistic sayings in the Gospel (amounting to about half of its total contents) may all be derived from the Gospel of the Egyptians, but (apart from the study of doublets) he offers no discussion of his conjecture. Even the more heterodox form of the doublets may, however, be ascribed to gnostic invention or editing rather than to an apocryphal source.[3]

In Saying 22 the disciples are told that they will enter the Kingdom 'when you make the two one, and when you make the inner as the outer and the above as the below, and when you make

[1] Rom. 2.29; Col. 2.11.
[2] *NT Apok.*, fr. 3, p. 108.
[3] Quispel, *VigChr* XI, 1957, p. 189.

the male and the female into a single one, so that the male will not be male and the female not be female'. There are close parallels in the writing known as *II Clement* (probably of Egyptian origin) and in Clement of Alexandria, who expressly refers to the Gospel of the Egyptians.[1] 'Neither male nor female' also occurs in the Naassene document and it is known that they made use of this apocryphal Gospel.[2] There is a somewhat similar theme in Saying 37, where the disciples are told that they will see our Lord 'when you take off your clothes and put them under your feet as the little children and tread on them'. The quotation given by Clement contains the phrase 'treading on the garment of shame' which echoes the same broad theme of contempt for and annulment of sex contained in the saying of Thomas. The transcendence of the contrast between male and female is the theme of Saying 114, which may well have the same origin. Salome, the interlocutor in Saying 61, certainly figured in this Gospel.[3] Indeed, the dialogue form seems to have been a notable feature of the Gospel of the Egyptians. We should not, however, on that count alone ascribe all similar material in the Gospel of Thomas to this source.

While the Gospel of the Hebrews seems to represent a specifically Jewish-Christian tradition probably not too markedly different from the canonical tradition, all that is known of the Gospel of the Egyptians is couched in a more riddling and cryptic form which plainly diverges from the broad stream of orthodox development. While the Jesus of the canonical Gospels is never afraid of paradox when it serves to make his meaning plain, he never descends to the level of obscurity almost for its own sake which characterizes what is known of this apocryphal Gospel. While it would be an exaggeration to speak of Egyptians as already gnostic, it is clearly already half-way towards gnosticism, and the tradition which it represents is already poised to take flight.[4] If this is a true estimate of the position, it becomes even more difficult to distinguish material in the Gospel of Thomas directly derived from this source from sayings actually composed

---

[1] *II Clem.* 12.2–6; Clement, *Strom.* 3.13, § 92.2.

[2] Hipp. *Ref.* 5.7.13–15; cf. 5.7.8.

[3] Clement, *Strom.* 3.9, § 63.1; *Exc. Theod.* 67.

[4] Gärtner, however, conjectures (p. 31) that the Gospel of the Egyptians may be gnostic, but admits that the evidence is not conclusive.

within gnosticism itself. Examples of this last group may be Sayings 13 (the promise to Thomas), 50 (possibly a piece of gnostic missionary apologetic) and 75 (the final stage of a developing logion).

The question whether the Gospel of Thomas was directly indebted to the canonical Gospels or used independent but closely related material is obviously a crucial question, and it would be idle to pretend that scholars are yet in a position to reach a definite conclusion. A strong case can be made out for both views, and the probabilities may even vary from saying to saying. The imposing list of New Testament parallels appended to the official translation does not settle the question. A more selective and informative list confined to the Gospels is contained in the edition by Grant and Freedman.[1]

So far as the Gospels are concerned parallels to Matthew and Luke predominate. Not unnaturally in his study of the parables Cerfaux finds Matthaean influence preponderant, since all the parables recorded in Matthew 13 are present in Thomas, though not all as Parables of the Kingdom.[2] Gärtner, however, does something to redress the balance with a careful note on Lucan influence in the Gospel.[3] Traces of Marcan influence are harder to determine. It is denied by Stead and Grant but claimed by Cerfaux that the Parable of the Mustard Seed is significantly closer to the version of Mark than that of the other Synoptists.[4] Other possible examples are to be found in Saying 21, where an allusion to Mark 4.29 (the Parable of the Seed Growing Secretly which is peculiar to Mark) seems probable, Saying 35 which only occurs as a direct statement in Mark and Saying 41.[5] The relative insignificance of Mark would be in line with the general tendency of the period as a whole.

As compared with the Synoptic Gospels the Fourth Gospel recedes into the background, but there is much to be said in favour of the view of Kasser that if the compiler appears to quote the Synoptists by preference, his style is formed on the Johannine

---

[1] Grant/Freedman, pp. 103 f.

[2] L. Cerfaux, *Muséon* LXX, 1957, p. 315; Wilson, *Studies*, pp. 53 f.

[3] Gärtner, pp. 66–68.

[4] G. C. Stead, 'New Gospel Discoveries', *Theology* LXII, 1959, p. 325; Grant/Freedman, p. 102.

[5] Cerfaux, *art. cit.*, pp. 311 f.

mould.[1] It is noteworthy that Johannine echoes are richer in those sayings which stand furthest from the canonical tradition. Other gnostics such as the Valentinians would show a marked preference for the Fourth Gospel.

While Quispel in particular presents a strong case for the independence of Thomas from the canonical tradition, recent scholars (such as Bartsch, Kasser, Gärtner and Grant and Freedman) tend to support the opposite view. After a close examination of individual sayings, Wilson concludes that, if in some cases the use of independent tradition is probable, direct indebtedness to the Gospel tradition is the most natural explanation of other sayings.

The problem is at least easy to state and leaps to the eye. On a liberal count there appear to be forty-four sayings in which canonical influence is probable.[2] While five sayings are virtually identical, most contain elements both of difference and similarity.[3] While runs of such sayings certainly occur, nothing in the arrangement or order of the Gospel suggests a consecutive following of a written source.[4] Thus the seven parables of Matt. 13 appear in the Gospel of Thomas as Sayings 9, 57, 20, 96, 109, 76 and 8.[5] Some sayings appear to be conflated from parallel versions in the synoptic tradition, while others are best explained as compound sayings containing allusions to material widely separated in the Gospel tradition. Both expansions and abbreviations of synoptic sayings occur. Certainly critics of the theory of indebtedness to the canonical tradition do not lack material within the Gospel of Thomas to support their view. Yet it may be doubted whether the difficulties are more successfully met on the rival theory. Appeal to lost sources contains inevitably a high degree of conjecture and gives no greater promise of solving the problem of the structure of the Gospel.

We must begin with the conditions of proof. The objection

---

[1] Grant, *VigChr* XIII, 1959, p. 176; Kasser, *RevThPh* 1959, p. 366.

[2] Sayings 5, 8 f., 14, 16, 20 f., 26, 31–36, 39, 41, 45–48, 54 f., 57, 63–66, 68 f., 72 f., 76, 78 f., 86, 89–91, 93 f., 96, 99 f., 107.

[3] Sayings 34 f., 41, 54, 73. Wilson, *Studies*, pp. 55 f.

[4] Six units (Sayings 31–36); four (Sayings 45–48, 63–66); three (Sayings 89–91; two (Sayings 20 f., 54 f., 56 f., 68 f., 72 f., 78 f., 93 f., 99 f.).

[5] Other examples of radical alteration of synoptic order can be found in the table in Grant/Freedman, pp. 103 f.

based upon the alterations of the order of synoptic material cannot be validly pressed in view of the miscellaneous character of the Gospel of Thomas. Quispel's theory that the compiler combined material drawn from the Gospels of the Hebrews and the Egyptians does not completely evade this difficulty and faces the additional problem of inferring the contents of two documents only preserved in scanty fragments. No convincing principle of the construction of Thomas has as yet emerged, although Kasser has outlined an interesting view that a basic gnostic hymn has been enlarged by the introduction of canonical and other material and worked up in a final gnostic revision. The development of this theory in fuller form will be awaited with interest. In some cases sayings appear to be arranged on the principle of community of ideas or of catchwords, while the Preamble and the first three sayings seem to be linked by a number of interlocking themes, the Living Jesus, the Kingdom, the All, the sons of the Living Father. The Gospel may be a *florilegium*, but even so the arrangement of material remains a problem on any showing. It may be recalled that the order of sayings within the Gospels themselves is not necessarily sacrosanct and the deliberate omission of incident in Thomas removes the chief pegs used for the combination of material in the canonical tradition.

A possible background for the production or compilation of conflated or compound sayings is sketched by Gärtner.[1] There is some evidence dating from the second century that the existence of the Fourfold Witness was regarded as an embarrassment rather than an enrichment. A Marcion or a Tatian would not have shared the robust confidence of St Irenaeus in the natural inevitability of four Gospels.[2] The combination of canonical material by orthodox writers (especially Clement and Origen) is not unknown. Notable examples are found in other gnostic writings as well as the Gospel of Thomas, and the charge levelled by St Irenaeus against the Valentinians that they broke up the mosaic and rearranged its components in different patterns clearly extended to other parts of the movement. The construction of gnostic targums employing canonical material could therefore be regarded as a reasonable procedure by contemporary standards.

---

[1] Gärtner, pp. 35–43.
[2] Iren., *Adv. haer.* 3.11.10 (II, pp. 46 f.).

Various motives might contribute to this process. Some units might be tendentious, convenient collections of proof texts for a given purpose. The example selected by Gärtner from the Clementine *Homilies* is a case in point.[1] But it might equally be 'neutral' with no clearly discernible motive. The result might be an associative or (as Gärtner calls it) a 'meditative' complex in which some echoes or allusions could be given in a word or two. Here a retentive or even a faulty memory might be at work. The introduction of subsidiary allusions could even appear to be an advantage at a period in which literal accuracy of quotation was not always of the first importance.

One particular method of quotation which appears in the Gospel of Thomas was current among the Naassenes.[2] It represents a curious tendency to invert the order of the canonical material. No convincing explanation for such an apparently irrational procedure has yet been discovered, but it may represent the gnostic claim that the Great Church had inverted the order of the Gospel. The key to the teaching of Jesus is given not to the ordinary catholic (the psychic) but to the gnostic believer (the pneumatic). Four clear examples occur in the Gospel of Thomas and will be treated here as evidence for a gnostic rather than a neutral treatment of the canonical material.

Of the sayings which concern us here six are virtually identical with synoptic material.[3] Five are clear cases of conflation of which three are concerned with the cost of discipleship and two are parables.[4] In neither case would there be great need to alter the content of the sayings, although gnostic tell-tales could be added with advantage. Thus Saying 16 introduces gnostic material at the conclusion of the synoptic logion, while Saying 99 makes a slight adaptation to the closing words of the original. In Saying 20 (the Parable of the Mustard Seed) the phrase 'the tilled earth' may hint at the prepared soul of the true gnostic. Saying 45 seems

---

[1] Gärtner, p. 40 n. 1, quoting Ps.-Clem. *Hom.* 19.2.

[2] Grant/Freedman, pp. 95, 100 f.

[3] Saying 34 (Matt. 15.14); 35 (Mark 3.27); 54 (Matt. 5.3, a tendentious revision); 73 (Luke 10.2); 41 (Mark 4.25, a neutral expansion).

[4] Saying 16: Matt. 10.34 f.; Luke 12.51–53 (Lucan preponderance); Saying 20: Mark 4.30–32; Matt. 13.31 f.; Luke 13.18 f. (Marcan preponderance); Saying 45: Matt. 6.16–19; Luke 6.43–45; Saying 55: Matt. 10.37 f.; Luke 14.26 f.; Saying 99: Mark 3.32–35; Matt. 12.49 f.; Luke 8.19–21.

completely neutral, while Saying 55 preserves the completely un-gnostic idea of taking up the cross of the original. Two other cases must be considered doubtful.[1]

Variations of synoptic order within a single saying or between consecutive sayings occur in a number of cases. Thus Sayings 92 and 93 represent Matt. 7.7 and 6. Saying 94 returns to Matt. 7.8. The opening words of Saying 14 allude to Matt. 6.16, 5 and 2 in that order. Saying 46 is based upon Matt. 11.12 and 11, while the succeeding logion combines Luke 6.39, 37 and 36. Finally Sayings 68–69 form a group of beatitudes approximating to Matt. 5.10, 8, and 6.

Compound sayings in the Gospel of Thomas are even more varied. Of these there are eleven instances, though two must be considered doubtful. While the whole group has a gnostic appli-cation, the hand of a gnostic compiler is particularly probable in five cases. Saying 79 combines Luke 11.27 f. and 23.29 in harmony with the gnostic depreciation of the body. Saying 39 opens with the denunciation of the Pharisees and scribes who have taken away the key of knowledge (Matt. 23.13; Luke 11.52), and con-cludes with the exhortation 'Become wise as serpents and harm-less as doves' (Matt. 10.16). A more complex procedure underlies the remaining sayings of this group. In two cases a gnostic provenance is suggested by a reversal of the order of the synoptic material. In the second half of Saying 21 two adjoining Lucan texts (Luke 12.39 and 35) are quoted in the reverse order and enriched by two slight but significant echoes derived from Mark (3.27 and 4.29). Saying 47 opens with an expanded but probably secondary version of Matt. 6.24 and Luke 16.13 (No man can serve two masters) and continues with the parable of the wine and the wineskins (Luke 5.36–39), where the sequence of the verses is reversed. The most complex example is Saying 14, concerned with religious observances. The first half has only slender connexions with the synoptic tradition. The practices are identical with those discussed in Matt. 6, but they are men-tioned in the reverse order. The second half concerns the ob-servance of food laws. It is based upon the Mission Charge to the Seventy in Luke 10.1–9, where the redundant command to heal

---

[1] Saying 26, where the Greek and Coptic versions differ widely; Saying 31, where an independent source may be more probable.

the sick makes the source reasonably certain. An additional argument against the practice is provided by a final allusion to Matt. 15.11.

Four examples bear less clear traces of gnostic compilation, though their appropriateness to gnostic teaching is not in doubt. Saying 33 combines material from Q (Matt. 10.27; Luke 12.3 and Matt. 5.15; Luke 11.13). In the second saying Lucan elements predominate. Saying 45 opens with a conflation of Matt. 7.16–19 and Luke 6.44 f., but ends with Matt. 12.35, a doublet of the preceding passage. In Saying 91 Luke 12.56 is obviously basic, but the question of the disciples either contains Johannine echoes or is cast in a Johannine mould. Traces of Matt. 16.1–3 have been less convincingly detected in the passage. A more complex example is Saying 76, of which the nucleus is to be found in a pair of parables in Matt. 13.45 f. (the Hid Treasure and the Pearl of Great Price). The former occurs as Saying 109 in Thomas as an independent unit probably derived from a non-canonical source. The compiler reverses the order of the Matthaean material and adds a Q saying about treasure (Matt. 6.20; Luke 12.33 f.) in compensation. Two subordinate echoes (John 6.27 and Mark 9.48) are introduced for good measure. The two doubtful cases are Saying 46 (based upon Matt. 11.12 and 11, where a subordinate allusion has been claimed to some such passage as Matt. 6.22 f. and Luke 11.34–36 in the cryptic and probably corrupt phrase 'so that his eyes shall be broken') and Saying 48 (the two in unity) where an extra-canonical source is more probable than the combination of some not very close synoptic parallels.

It is not difficult to account for the selection of this block of material on gnostic premises. In common with other gnostic documents the parables are heavily represented.[1] Sayings of our Lord which could be held to imply a deeper teaching hidden from the ordinary believer and demanding special gifts of perception are laid under contribution.[2] The synoptic contrasts between Light and Darkness, Sight and Blindness came readily to hand.[3] The gnostic is the man of understanding or the child who knows the kingdom.[4] Gnosis itself is the good treasure, the good fruit

[1] Sayings 8 f., 20, 57, 63–65, 76, 96, 107.
[2] Sayings 5, 20, 33, 39, 93.
[3] Sayings 26, 32–34.
[4] Sayings 21, 46.

or the new wine.[1] It is the promised 'rest' and the gnostic is the true heir of the Gospel beatitudes.[2] It demands an undivided allegiance. Gnostic no less than Gospel discipleship is at cost and may involve persecution.[3] The gnostic cannot expect to be acceptable to his own kith and kin, nor will the kings and great ones of the earth be of his company.[4] The inward way of gnostic mysticism can afford to dispense with ordinary religious observances.[5] It involves the renunciation of the body and its works and leads to victory over the world.[6] Synoptic teaching about the Kingdom is retained, but revalued in harmony with gnostic mysticism. It is inward and spiritual; God's moment (καιρός) cannot be tested, for no outward manifestation of its coming can be seen. Synoptic watchfulness becomes gnostic insight.[7] These themes are not, of course, confined to this group of sayings; indeed, they are amply illustrated by the rest of the collection.

Some indications of gnostic editorial activity have already been noted in the discussion of conflates and compound sayings. It will only be necessary to give some further examples and to discuss its methods. In Saying 100 the background of the incident of the Tribute Money is lightly sketched, but the concluding logion is expanded into a threefold form: 'Give the things of Caesar to Caesar, give the things of God to God and give me what is mine.'[8] Here an allusion to the three natures of mankind and their celestial counterparts may be suspected. The consistent avoidance of the word 'God' in connexion with the Kingdom and the alteration of the Lucan form of the first Lucan beatitude in Saying 54 strongly suggests that for Thomas God denotes the Demiurge. The slight variants at the beginning of the Parable of the Sower (Saying 9) might be interpreted not as indications of an extra-canonical source but as a deliberate twist to the story to indicate that the Sower is not our Lord but the Demiurge. The parable is

[1] Sayings 45, 76, 47.
[2] Rest: Sayings 86, 90; beatitude: Sayings 54, 68 f.
[3] Cost of discipleship: Sayings 16, 47, 55, 72; persecution: Sayings 66, 68 f.
[4] Sayings 16, 55, 99 and 78.
[5] Sayings 89, 14.
[6] Renunciation of the body: Sayings 36, 79; victory over the world: Sayings 21, 35.
[7] Sayings 20 f., 46, 79, 91, 96, 99, 107.
[8] Mark 12.13–17; Matt. 22.16–21; Luke 20.21–25.

here not described as a Parable of the Kingdom and it is known that other gnostics interpreted it in this sense. Other slight alterations to parables and sayings may be designed to accentuate the status of the gnostic believer. He is the 'large and good fish', the 'tilled earth', the 'large loaf', the 'gold coin' and the 'large sheep'.[1] This form of theological italics may be too significant of gnostic *amour propre* to be satisfactorily explained either as neutral expansions or indications of a difference of source. In Saying 72, which depends directly upon Luke 12.14, extensive editorial revision has clearly taken place. The gnostic application is made clear at the start. 'My father's possessions' points to gnostic beatitude. Our Lord is no longer the 'judge' either to lay additional emphasis upon what for the gnostic was the main point of the story or as a concept not easily assimilable to his theology. The concluding question 'I am not a divider, am I?' is interpreted by Quispel and Gershenson as 'schismatic' in the light of some early Jewish-Christian evidence.[2] This seems over-subtle, and a less technical interpretation is probably to be preferred. The saying suggests that the gnostic way of unity will be attended by division. In Saying 90 a process of judicious omission combined with a subtle change of emphasis in the final clause converts a Gospel promise into a piece of gnostic spirituality. It is no longer addressed to the weary and heavy-laden, and the 'rest' is no longer a divine gift but a matter of gnostic attainment. The gnostic undervaluation of the body is given a foothold in the synoptic tradition in two opposite ways. In Saying 79 a new compound is constructed out of two Lucan passages in which the second (taken out of its context) is used to establish the meaning of the first, while in Saying 36 the Coptic text makes a drastic cut in the Greek version of Thomas and the synoptic source in order to emphasize the point. More frequently the gnostic editor contents himself with adding gnostic material at the end of a synoptic saying or with making a slight adaptation of its concluding phrase.[3] If the existence of gnostic editing of Gospel material appears probable, its extent must remain a matter of conjecture. Some apparently neutral redactions may well have

[1] Sayings 8, 20, 96, 100, 107.
[2] G. Quispel and D. Gershenson, 'Meristae', *VigChr* XII, 1958, pp. 19–26.
[3] Cf., for example, Sayings 16, 69a, 78, 86, 99.

had a gnostic intention, but the absence of a precise theological context for the new sayings makes a measure of caution advisable.

A strong case can therefore be made out for the direct dependence of a number of sayings in the Gospel of Thomas upon the canonical tradition. Some light is shed upon divergences from the standard text by gnostic methods of exegesis and particular gnostic patterns of doctrine and spirituality. It reduces the extent of appeal to lost sources which must inevitably remain unknown quantities and therefore has some claim to be regarded as the most economical hypothesis. It cannot, however, in the present stage of discussion be regarded as established beyond doubt, and the main alternative view proposed by Quispel will no doubt continue to receive support. The gap between them may not even be as great as might be thought, since those who claim direct dependence upon the canonical tradition do not exclude the use of extra-canonical material in other parts of the Gospel, while those who regard this theory as unproved admit that so far as an important block of material is concerned their non-canonical source is not markedly divergent from the Gospel tradition of the Great Church.

II

A COMPARISON OF THE PARABLES OF THE GOSPEL ACCORDING TO THOMAS AND OF THE SYNOPTIC GOSPELS

HOWEVER interesting 'The Gospel according to Thomas'[1] may be to students of the primitive Church, it seems at first sight highly improbable that this strange farrago of sayings will make any contribution to our knowledge of Jesus' teaching. And yet to the New Testament scholar the Gospel according to Thomas is perhaps the most interesting of all the manuscripts found near Nag Hammadi in 1945, inasmuch as some of its contents have affinities with the sayings and parables of Jesus which are found in the canonical Gospels. A comparison of the parables and similitudes found in Thomas with parallel material in the Synoptic Gospels[2] raises fascinating and fundamental problems of higher criticism.

[1] For English translations, *The Gospel According to Thomas*, ed. and translated by A. Guillaumont, H. Ch. Puech, G. Quispel, W. Till and Yassah 'abd Al Masīḥ, 1959; R. M. Grant and D. N. Freedman, *The Secret Sayings of Jesus*, 1960 [cited as Grant/Freedman]; for a French translation, J. R. Doresse, *Les Paroles de Jésus* (Paris, 1959) [cited as Doresse]; for a German translation, J. Leipoldt, 'Ein neues Evangelium?', *TLZ* LXXXIII, 1958, pp. 481 ff.; for a Latin translation, G. Garitte, *Muséon* LXX, 1957, pp. 59 ff. In this article I have made use of both English translations and occasionally I have made my own alterations with the kind assistance of Professor J. M. Plumley. As the system of numeration differs from translation to translation, I have cited the text by reference to the plates and lines of the photographic edition of the text in *Coptic Gnostic Papyri in the Coptic Museum at Old Cairo*, ed. P. Labib, vol. I (Cairo, 1956) (shown in the margin of both English translations).

[2] Sayings from M, L, and Q can be paralleled in Thomas, as well as some sayings common to all three Synoptics. It is therefore necessary to assume either that Thomas used Matthew and Luke (and possibly Mark) or that he had access to sources which contained some sayings similar to those found in M, L, Q and Mark. The fact that Thomas occasionally has some details in agreement with Mark against Matthew and Luke as well as points in common with Matthew and Luke against Mark does not prove that Thomas must be dependent on the Synoptic Gospels.

Three possible hypotheses may be put forward to account for these similarities:

1. Thomas may have been dependent on the Synoptic Gospels and he may have used them as a kind of quarry from which he excavated some of his material rough hewn before he shaped it to his purpose.[1]
2. Thomas may have relied on his own reminiscences of the canonical Gospels without using these Gospels as written sources.
3. Thomas may have used other sources which were independent of the Synoptic Gospels, but which contained some similar material.[2]

These three hypotheses are probably mutually exclusive. If had the text of the Synoptic Gospels in front of him when he composed his sayings collection, it is improbable that he also cited from memory sayings from the Synoptic Gospels.[3] Similarly, if Thomas made use of sources independent of the Synoptic Gospels but containing some similar material, it is unlikely that he at the same time used the Synoptic Gospels as a source; for it is extremely difficult on this hypothesis to account for Thomas's disuse of synoptic material which would have been so well suited to his gnostic purposes. For the same reason it is improbable that Thomas combined his own reminiscences of the canonical Gospels with other written sources.

The existence of doublets in the text of Thomas is relevant to a consideration of its sources. These doublets represent different

---

[1] R. Kasser, 'Les Manuscrits de Nag-Hammadi: faits, documents, problèmes', *RevThPh*, 1959, p. 364, declares that on closer inspection Thomas's dependence on the Synoptic Gospels 'appears more and more evident'; while H. K. McArthur (*ExpT* LXXI 1960, p. 286) asserts that Thomas is, 'demonstrably dependent on the Synoptics'.

[2] J. Leipoldt (*art. cit.*, pp. 494 ff.) holds that Thomas uses a current of Synoptic tradition independent of the canonical Gospels. G. Quispel concludes that Thomas contains 'an independent and very old Gospel tradition' ('Some Remarks on the Gospel of Thomas', *NTS* V, 1959, p. 277). Many scholars are more cautious; e.g. W. C. van Unnik opines that this 'is not an *a priori* impossibility' (*Newly Discovered Gnostic Writings*, p. 56).

[3] Thomas's material may be divided into four categories: (i) sayings identical or nearly identical with logia found in the canonical Gospels; (ii) sayings which have some kinship with logia found in the canonical Gospels; (iii) sayings with a Jewish-Christian background; (iv) sayings with a gnostic background. It is not impossible that sayings in category (i) have been derived from the Synoptic Gospels, while those in category (ii) have been taken from an independent source or sources.

stages of development in the tradition of a particular saying.[1] If a compiler is citing sayings from memory, either at random or by word association, he is very unlikely to quote two different versions of the same saying. But if he is compiling a work from two or more written sources, he may either conflate two similar versions, or prefer one to the other, or quote both. The fact that two different versions of the same saying are at times cited by Thomas makes it so probable that he was compiling his collection from *written* sources that the hypothesis of 'memory citation' will be disregarded in the remainder of this chapter. It will be assumed that Thomas was either using the Synoptic Gospels as his source, or that he was using a source or sources which were independent of the Synoptic Gospels, but which contained some parallel material. Two of Thomas's doublets have no relationship to synoptic material.[2] The five remaining doublets although they are not identical with synoptic parallels, have some kinship with them.[3] The fact that none of these doublets exactly reproduces a synoptic saying makes it improbable that Thomas was using the Synoptic Gospels as a source: but this view needs to be tested by a comparison of the parallel material.

The Gospel according to Thomas was evidently put together by a gnosticizing Christian. Probably it was used, as Cerfaux has suggested, in Valentinian circles.[4] The teaching that it contains has affinities with that of the Valentinian gnostics,[5] the Naassenes,[6]

---

[1] Cf. doublets in Matthew and Luke which show the overlapping of Mark and Q, e.g. 'taking up the cross', for which Matt. 16.24 and Luke 9.23 reproduce Mark 8.34, while Matt. 10.38 and Luke 14.27 represent the Q tradition. (Cf. B. H. Streeter, *The Four Gospels*, 1936, p. 191.) Thomas records a further version of this saying (90.25–29).

[2] (i) The World a Corpse (90.30–32; 95.12–14); (ii) Body and Soul (96.4–7; 99.10–12).

[3] (i) The Kingdom of God is within (Thomas 80.19–26; 99.14–18; cf. Luke 17.20); (ii) I Came to Cast Fire (Thomas 82.14–16; 83.32–36; cf. Luke 12.49, 51; Matt. 10.34); (iii) Hating one's Family (Thomas 90.25–29; 97.32–36; cf. Matt. 10.37; Luke 14.26); (iv) The Parable of the Robber (Thomas 85.7–10; 98.6–10; cf. Matt. 24.43 f.; Luke 12.39 f.); (v) Power to Move Mountains (Thomas 89.24–26; 98.18–22; cf. Matt. 18.19; 17.20; Mark 11.23).

[4] L. Cerfaux, 'Les Parables du Royaume', *Muséon* LXX, 1957, p. 322.

[5] Irenaeus, *Adv. haer.* 1.20.2, attributes to Marcosian gnostics a saying similar to Thomas 88.2–5. The idea that a woman should become a man (Thomas 99.22) is attributed to the Valentinian gnostic Theodotus (Clement, *Exc. Theod.* 21.3).

[6] Many similarities can be noted between Thomas and the Naassene

and the Basilidean gnostics.[1] It was rejected by Origen,[2] Eusebius of Caesarea[3] and Cyril of Jerusalem (although Cyril is wrong in ascribing it to the Manichaeans,[4] for it was in existence before them). Augustine rejects an *agraphon* (found in Thomas) as apocryphal and fictitious.[5] However, the fact that a work has strong affinities with gnostic thought does not necessarily mean that its sources are tainted.

The Coptic manuscript of Thomas found at Khenoboskion was written sometime between the second half of the third and the fifth centuries AD.[6] But Thomas had been in existence in a Greek text no later than the early third century AD, as the Oxyrhynchus papyri show.[7] A comparison of the relevant Oxyrhynchus fragments with the text of the Coptic manuscript does not show many

---

gnostics: (i) *Androgyneity* to which Thomas refers so often (81.10; 85.25, 29; 86.3; 89.28; 94.12; 98.19) is found in Naassene thought (Hipp. *Ref.* 5.7.14); (ii) *Stripping Naked* which is mentioned in the Parable of the Children in the Field (Thomas 85.4; cf. 87.31 f.) finds an echo in Hipp. *Ref.* 5.8.44; (iii) *The Three Secret Words*, mentioned by Hipp. *Ref.* 5.8.5 seem to be intended in Thomas 83.8; (iv) A saying about *The Living and The Dead* which is found in Thomas 82.19–22 has a parallel in Hipp. *Ref.* 5.8.32; (v) According to Hipp. *Ref.* 5.7.1; 10.9.3, the Naassene traditions were handed down from James the Just through Mariamme. Mariamme is also connected with the Naassenes in *Acts of Philip* 94 ff. She is mentioned in Thomas 84.34; 99.19 (Mariham), and James the Just is the subject of a saying in Thomas 82.29; (vi) a saying about *A Child of Seven Years* is actually attributed to the Gospel of Thomas in connexion with the Naassenes in Hipp. *Ref.* 5.7.20. It appears, however, in a very different form in Thomas 81.5–8, and on the strength of this difference Puech almost went so far as to deny any direct connexion between our Gospel of Thomas and the gospel used by the Naassenes (H. Ch. Puech, 'L'évangile selon Thomas', *Comptes Rendus de l'Academie des Inscriptions et Belles-Lettres* (1957), p. 151). R. M. Grant ('Notes on the Gospel of Thomas', *VigChr* XIII, 1959, p. 178) adduces further connexions with the Naassene gnostics.

[1] Irenaeus, *Adv. haer.* 1.24.6, discussing the tenets of the Basilidean gnostics, uses similar words to those found in Thomas 86.2. R. M. Grant (*art. cit.*, 172 f.) suggests other parallels between Thomas and the Basilideans.

[2] *Hom. in Luc.* 1.

[3] *Hist. eccl.* 3.25.6.

[4] *Catech.* 4.36; 6.31.

[5] *C. advers. legis et prophetarum* 2.4, 14; cf. Thomas, 90.16–18.

[6] Cf. H. Ch. Puech, *op. cit.*, pp. 148 f.

[7] Grenfell and Hunt regarded Pap. Oxy. 1 as 'probably written not much later than the year 200' (*Sayings of Our Lord from an Early Greek Papyrus* [1897], p. 6); Pap. Oxy. 654 in 'the middle or end of the third century' (*New*

differences, but the divergencies, such as they are, are significant. It seems probable that, sometime between the Greek and the Coptic versions, Thomas had been altered in a gnosticizing direction.[1]

It is difficult to decide with certainty the place from which Thomas first emanated, but such indications as there are point towards Syria. For the opening words of Thomas speak of 'Didymus Judas Thomas'. Thomas is regularly called Judas Thomas by the Eastern fathers and in oriental apocrypha,[2] but only in the *Acts of Thomas* can the phrase Judas Thomas Didymus be found.[3] The fact that the *Acts of Thomas* probably emanated from Edessa near the beginning of the third century[4] points towards Syria as the place of origin of the Gospel of Thomas. Furthermore, it is in an old Syrian manuscript that Judas Thomas is found instead of the simple Thomas at John 14.22.[5] Moreover, in the Gospel of Thomas, the person of Thomas the Apostle is so exalted that he is the recipient of a special revelation from Jesus;[6] and it is in the Syrian *Acts of Thomas* that Thomas is described as the twin brother of Jesus himself,[7] and the recipient of a special revelation.[8] It seems probable, therefore, that the Gospel of

---

Sayings of Jesus and Fragment of a Lost Gospel [1904], p. 9); Pap. Oxy. 655 'not likely to have been written later than AD 250' (*op. cit.*, p. 37). These Oxyrhynchus papyri were first connected with the Coptic Gospel of Thomas by Puech in 1954, and Fitzmyer has described them as 'all parts of the same work: they represent three different copies of the Greek text at different times and give evidence of a fairly frequent copying of it in the third century AD.' (J. A. Fitzmyer, 'The Oxyrhynchus *Logoi* of Jesus and the Coptic Gospel According to Thomas', *Theological Studies* XX, 1959, p. 510).

[1] Cf. Grant/Freedman, p. 68. H. Ch. Puech suggests that Thomas was current in at least two recensions, one of which was used in orthodox and the other in gnostic circles (*NT Apok.*, pp. 221 f.). Gärtner, however, believes that 'the majority of differences are due to the carelessness of the translator' (p. 87).

[2] Cf. Doresse, p. 40.
[3] *Acta Thomae*, 1.
[4] Cf. Doresse, p. 44.
[5] Nitriensis. Cf. W. C. van Unnik, *op. cit.*, p. 49.
[6] 83.7 ff.
[7] *Acta Thomae*, 11.
[8] *Acta Thomae*, 39.

Thomas was first composed in Syria not later than the end of the second century AD.

If the hypothesis that Thomas is not dependent on the Synoptic Gospels is examined, the existence of other sources containing material similar to the canonical Gospels must be investigated. What sources would have been available to a writer between AD 150 and 200? The Gospel to the Hebrews was certainly in existence by the earlier date.[1] Only fragments of this Gospel are extant.[2] It is interesting that Clement of Alexandria on one occasion cites an *agraphon* as though it belonged to Scripture,[3] while on another occasion he quotes the same *agraphon* in a slightly different form, giving the Gospel to the Hebrews as its origin.[4] This *agraphon* (again in slightly different forms) can be found both in the Oxyrhynchus fragment of Thomas[5] and in the Coptic manuscript of the Gospel.[6] It is therefore extremely probable that Thomas did make use of the Gospel of the Hebrews.[7]

Thomas also has affinities with the Gospel to the Egyptians. This also was in existence before the end of the second century, for Clement of Alexandria quotes from it.[8] Another citation of Clement[9] has its counterparts in the Gospel of Thomas,[10] and although it is difficult to determine the precise relationship here between Thomas and the Gospel to the Egyptians,[11] it is probable that the former made use of the latter. Both were current in Egypt.

Here, then, are two possible sources which Thomas may have used in compiling his sayings collection. He may have used other

---

[1] It was known to Irenaeus (*Adv. haer.* 1.26.2; 3.11.7) as well as to Clement.
[2] Cf. M. R. James, *The Apocryphal New Testament*, 1924, pp. 1 ff.; *NT Apok.*, p. 97.
[3] *Strom.* 5.14, § 96.3.
[4] *Strom.* 2.9, § 45.5.
[5] Pap. Oxy. 654, second saying.
[6] Thomas 80.15–19.
[7] A further indebtedness to the Gospel of the Hebrews may be found in Thomas 98.12 f., 'What sin have I committed?' (cf. Jerome, *Dial. adv. Pelag.* 3.2).
[8] Concerning a conversation between Jesus and Salome (*Strom.* 3.9, § 63.3; cf. Thomas 91.30 ff.).
[9] *Strom.* 3.13, § 93.2.
[10] Thomas 85.23–35; 87.29–88.1.
[11] The problem is rendered complex by cognate *agrapha* in *II Clem.* 12.2 and *Mart. Petri* 9 (Lipsius and Bonnet I, p. 94).

sources also.[1] Since practically nothing is known about the contents of the Gospels to the Hebrews and to the Egyptians, it is impossible to determine the extent of Thomas's indebtedness to either. The possibility can, however, no longer be excluded that Thomas derived none of his material from the Synoptic Gospels: he may have taken from the Gospels to the Hebrews and to the Egyptians[2] those of his sayings which have their counterpart in the Synoptic Gospels. If he did not use the Synoptic Gospels, it seems probable that he derived his parallel material from the Gospel to the Hebrews rather than from the Gospel to the Egyptians, for two reasons. In the first place the Gospel to the Hebrews is known to have contained early tradition and it is more likely to have overlapped with the Synoptic Gospels than the Gospel to the Egyptians; for what is known about the latter leads to the supposition that it was a gnosticizing work. Secondly, some differences between Thomas and the Synoptic Gospels can be explained on the hypothesis that they both derive from a common Aramaic tradition; and Hebrews was written in Aramaic.[3]

It is only the parables and similitudes of Thomas that will here

[1] The saying in Thomas 94.9–11, 'O Lord there are many about the well but there are none in the well' was known to Celsus (Origen, *c. Cels.* 8.15 f.). The logion in Thomas 95.17–19, 'He who is near me is near the fire and he who is far from me is far from the Kingdom', was known to Origen, who even thought that it might be authentic (*Hom. in Jerem.* 20.3). (Cf. J. Jeremias, *The Unknown Sayings of Jesus*, 1957, pp. 54 ff.) A logion similar to Thomas 89.24–26 is found in *Didascalia Apostolorum* 15 (Connolly, p. 134). The words in Thomas 84.17 f., 'Blessed is he who was before he came into being', are found in Irenaeus, *Dem. ev. apost.* 43. Reminiscences of Thomas 86.17–20 may be found in Justin, *Dial c. Tryph.* 12.3 and Irenaeus, *op. cit.* 96 ('truly keeping the sabbath') and in Clement, *Strom.* 3.15, § 99.4 ('fasting from the world'). The sources of all these sayings are unknown. H. Ch. Puech (*NT Apok.*, pp. 216 ff.) has listed eighteen logia which are quoted or to which allusions are made in patristic, gnostic or Manichean writings.

[2] H. Ch. Puech ('L'évangile selon Thomas', *Comptes Rendus de l'Academie des Inscriptions et Belles-Lettres*, 1957, p. 160.), W. Till (*BJRL* XLI, 1958/9, p. 451), and G. Quispel (*VigChr* XI, 1957, p. 194) are of the opinion that the Gospels to the Hebrews and the Egyptians lie behind the Gospel according to Thomas.

[3] Quispel has pointed out some variants in Thomas similar to those in Jewish-Christian literature ('L'évangile selon Thomas et les Clementines', *VigChr* XII, 1958, pp. 181–96). He had also pointed out similarities between Thomas and some versions of the Diatessaron (The Gospel of Thomas and the New Testament, *VigChr* XI, 1957, pp. 187–207), and he has further adduced readings from the ninth-century *Heliand*, which was itself based on the Diatessaron ('Some remarks on the Gospel of Thomas', *NTS* V, 1959,

be examined and compared with synoptic parallels. This selection
has been made because the parables and similitudes form a
manageable unit of comparison and because many of the more
striking similarities can be found in them. Furthermore, if the
general tendency of New Testament scholarship over the last
twenty-five years has been to retreat from the quest of the
historical Jesus, the study of the Gospel parables provides a conspicuous and welcome exception. If the outline of Jesus' ministry
becomes in the opinion of scholars more and more obscure, yet
it would seem that the words and the point of the Gospel parables,
as spoken by Jesus, are becoming clearer and clearer. Ever since
Jülicher published his epoch-making book, *Die Gleichnisreden
Jesu*,[1] a clear evolution of thought concerning the interpretation
of the Gospel parables can be discerned.[2] Interpretation has shifted
from allegory to stories which illustrate general principles, and
thence to stories which depict a concrete situation analogous to a
situation confronting Jesus or those with whom he came into
contact. We have moved from allegorical to existentialist interpretation of the parables. Jeremias's book, *The Parables of Jesus*,[3]
would seem to be the end-term of this development. Jeremias
enumerates what he calls 'laws of transformation'[4] and what
would better be described as 'tendencies towards alteration'. It

---

pp. 283 f.). Centuries ago it was surmised that Tatian composed his Diatessaron not from four but from five gospels; and the fifth may have been the
Gospel to the Hebrews. Thus similarities between Thomas, the Clementine
literature and some versions of the Diatessaron might be explained by their
common dependence on the Gospel to the Hebrews. A. Guillaumont ('Sémi-
tismes dans les logia de Jesus retrouvés à Nag-Hammadi', *Journal Asiatique*
CCXLVI, 1958, pp. 113–23) has joined with Quispel in carrying the argument one stage further. Many such variants show evidence of primitive
Aramaisms and some can be explained by reference to a supposed Aramaic
tradition being behind the synoptic versions. If this argument is accepted,
it can be held that Thomas is dependent on an Aramaic source (probably
translated into Greek in the second century) which is independent of the
Synoptic Gospels.

[1] Vol. I, Tübingen, 1888; vol. II, 1899.
[2] Cf. A. T. Cadoux, *The Parables of Jesus, Their Art and Use* (1931); T. W.
Manson, *The Teaching of Jesus* (1935); C. H. Dodd, *The Parables of the Kingdom*
(1935); W. O. E. Oesterley, *The Gospel Parables in the Light of their Jewish
Background* (1936); B. T. D. Smith, *The Parables of the Synoptic Gospels* (1937).
[3] ET, 1954.
[4] *Op. cit.*, p. 88.

is instructive to compare the parables and similitudes in Thomas with parallel sayings in the Synoptic Gospels, using Jeremias's principles of criticism.

I. EMBELLISHMENT

Jeremias[1] noted a tendency for the Gospel parables to be embellished as they became further removed from their historical origin in the words of Jesus.

In Thomas's version of the Sower, the good seed is said to bear fruit 'sixty per measure and a hundred and twenty per measure' (82.13). Mark and Matthew, however, have variations on the theme of thirty, sixty and a hundred (Mark 4.20; Matt. 13.23): Luke has only a hundred fold (Luke 8.8). Triplets are more common that doublets in Jewish writing and numbers tend to increase rather than decrease. Possibly Thomas wrote 'a hundred and twenty' because twelve is the number of completion.[2]

An interesting instance of embellishment can be seen in Thomas's version of the Banquet. Matthew has three categories of guests who refused the invitation, one who went to his field, another to his merchandise and 'the rest' (Matt. 22.5 f.). Luke also mentions three categories of guests; one who had bought a field, a second who had bought a yoke of oxen and a third who had just got married (Luke 14.18–20). Thomas, however, has four sets of excuses (92.14–29). Again, triplets are more common

---

[1] *Op. cit.*, pp. 21 ff.

[2] Thomas records, like Luke (8.6), that some seed fell on rock (contrast Mark 4.5 and Matt. 13.5, 'rocky ground'). Thomas does not mention either Mark's or Matthew's shallowness of soil and heat of the sun or Luke's lack of moisture. Other differences may be more significant. There may be a Semitizing asyndeton in 'The sower went out, he filled his hand, he threw' (82.4 f.). 'The worm ate them' (82.10) may be the original description of what happened to the choked seed. According to Thomas some seed fell 'on the road' (82.5), while the synoptics read παρὰ τὴν ὁδόν. The synoptic version is rather puzzling: there were no pavements in first-century Palestine and men walked on the path. 'On the road' is found in Ps.-Clement. *Recog.* (syr. and lat.) 3.14 as well as in the Aramaic Diatessaron (cf. G. Quispel, *VigChr* XII, 1958, pp. 183 f.). Quispel further points out (*NTS* V, 1959, p. 285) that the same variant is found in Justin (*Dial. c. Tryph.* 125) as well as in the *Heliand* (line 2388). It is possible that these represent a Jewish Christian tradition stemming, like the synoptic παρὰ τὴν ὁδόν, from the original Aramaic *al urḥa*. H. W. Bartsch, however, believes that Thomas here reflects a correction of the synoptic tradition ('Das Thomas-Evangelium und die synoptischen Evangelien', *NTS* VI, 1960, pp. 250 f.).

than quadruplets. Furthermore, three of Thomas's invited guests say: 'I pray have me excused.' But the man who says that he has bought a house and who has been requested for a day would not say this. It seems probable that here also is an embellishment.

However, the criterion of embellishment, as Jeremias admits, must be used 'with great caution'.[1] In the Parable of the Patch, he suggests[2] that the Lucan version is an embellishment of Mark and that the former version loses punch because the point about the rent being made worse by repair has been lost (Luke 5.36; contrast Mark 2.21). In Thomas's version, however, there is a saying not about a new patch on an old garment but about an old patch on a new garment (89.22 f.).[3] It is possible that Luke's version is not so much an embellishment of Mark as a conflation of both Mark and the tradition behind Thomas.[4]

Another example of possible embellishment can be seen in Thomas's version of the Parable of the Vineyard (93.1–16). Here the owner of the vineyard makes excuses for the bad treatment accorded to his first envoy: 'Perhaps he did not know them' (93.9). But there seems no point in this addition, except that it accords with Thomas's statement (which is not paralleled elsewhere) that the owner of the vineyard was 'a good man' (93.1). It seems probable that, far from being additions to the story, these details were originally part of the parable.[5] On the other hand, Thomas omits to make it clear that the owner of the vineyard was an absentee landlord. According to Jeremias, it is only when a proselyte dies intestate that the tenants of his property may gain possession of it.[6] But it is hardly necessary to imagine that the original story turned on a nice point of law. It seems that

---

[1] *Parables*, p. 22.

[2] *Ibid.*

[3] Grant/Freedman's suggestion that Thomas has changed the synoptic reading 'because he is thinking of life in the new world' (p. 150) is not very convincing. Quispel points out that Thomas's reading is attested by the Persian Diatessaron (*VigChr* XI, 1957, p. 194).

[4] This suggestion is made by Quispel (*NTS* V, 1959, p. 281).

[5] Instead of the synoptic 'let it out' (ἐξέδετο, Mark 12.1 *et par.*) Thomas has 'so that they would work it and that he would receive its fruit' (93.3). This is no more than a clumsy periphrasis.

[6] *Op. cit.*, p. 59. The point is contested by E. Bammel ('Das Gleichnis von den bösen Winzern', *Revue Internationale des Droits de l'Antiquité* VI, 1959, pp. 11 ff.).

the labourers in the parable were the kind of people who believed that possession is nine-tenths of the law; and Thomas's version assumes that the owner of the vineyard lived away from his property.

There are times when it is hard to decide whether Thomas embellishes a parable or retains a more original version than the Synoptic Gospels. For example, in the Parable of the Pearl the merchant according to Matthew was a dealer in pearls (Matt. 13.45); but according to Thomas he was a general merchant with an eye for a good bargain (94.15). The parable gains in point if it depicts the latter; and probably Thomas here retains an authentic point. Again, in the Parable of the Lost Sheep, Matthew and Luke tell a story about simply 'a man' (Matt. 18.12; Luke 15.4), but Thomas describes 'a shepherd' (98.23). Is Thomas adding a detail or has the Q version omitted it? Furthermore, in Thomas the shepherd tires himself out looking for the lost sheep (98.26). Neither Matthew nor Luke include this detail, although Luke states that the man carried back the sheep on his shoulders (Luke 15.6). Once again, it seems probable that Thomas retains here an authentic touch.

On the other hand, there are some parables in Thomas which are less vivid than their parallels in the canonical Gospels, and it seems probable that they have lost some of their original details. For example, the Parable of the Rich Fool in Thomas lacks some of the striking details of the Lucan parallel (92.2–10; contrast Luke 12.16–21), for the Rich Fool's conversation with himself is not so intimate and Thomas lacks the word of doom from God which is found in Luke: 'Thou fool, this night thy soul shall be required of thee: then whose shall those things be, which thou hast provided?' (Luke 12.20).[1] The Lucan version is here to be preferred. Similarly the Parable of the Leaven is compressed in its Q form (Matt. 13.31 f.; Luke 13.20 f.), but in Thomas it is even more compressed (97.2–6), and it is not there recorded that the woman took three measures of barley. Dalman has pointed out that this should have been sufficient to provide bread for 162 persons.[2] This detail was probably authentic:

---

[1] G. C. Stead comments: 'flat stuff by comparison' ('New Gospel Discoveries', *Theology* LXII, 1959, p. 326).
[2] Cf. Jeremias, *op. cit.*, p. 90 n. 4.

numbers tend to drop out as a story is retold.[1] Again, the Parable of the Mustard Seed in Thomas (84.28 ff.) is more compressed than the Marcan and Matthaean versions (Mark 4.30–32; Matt. 13.31 f.). Thomas, by abbreviating the parable, has omitted Old Testament allusions which even Luke retains in his abbreviated version (Luke 13.18 f.).[2] Thus according to Thomas the tree becomes a shelter for the birds of heaven: the synoptic versions, following Ezekiel, record that it provides shade, and that the birds nest beneath its shade. Thomas also fails to make the point which is found in all three Synoptic Gospels that the mustard seed becomes larger than all the trees. (Cf. Luke's version of Mark: Luke omits to record that the mustard seed is the smallest of all the seeds.) A second instance of Thomas's failure to keep Old Testament allusions is to be found in his version of the Parable of the Vineyard. All three Synoptic Gospels have at least some allusion to Isa. 5.1 f. (Mark 12.1; Matt. 21.33; Luke 20.9). Thomas, however, merely reads: 'A good man had a vineyard' (93.1). It is probable that the Isaianic allusion was part of the original parable:[3] Thomas's attitude to the Old Testament tends to be negative.[4]

Thomas's version of the Tares and the Wheat provides a striking instance of compression to the point of absurdity,[5] and in this respect Thomas's version is plainly inferior to Matthew (90.33–91.7; Matt. 13.24–30).[6] Thomas differs from Matthew as

[1] A further instance of compression is seen in Thomas's version of the Parable of the Mote and the Beam (Thomas 86.12–17; cf. Matt. 7.3–5; Luke 6.41 f.) Here R. McL. Wilson suggests that 'a case might be made out for expansion in the canonical tradition' (*Studies*, p. 58).

[2] Ezek. 17.23; 31.6; Dan. 4.12.

[3] Wilson suggests, however, that the Isaianic quotation may be a Marcan or pre-Marcan addition (*op. cit.*, p. 102).

[4] A further example of Thomas's disuse of Old Testament allusions can be seen in his logion about family strife. Thomas 83.36–84.3 is further away from Micah 7.6 than the synoptic versions in Matt. 10.35 and Luke 12.52 f. Occasionally Thomas includes an Old Testament allusion which is not found in the Synoptic Gospels ('guard him as the apple of thine eye', Thomas 86.11 f.; cf. Ps. 17.8 etc.). However, Thomas's attitude to the Old Testament seems to be summed up in 90.13–18: 'His disciples said to him: Twenty-four prophets spoke in Israel and they all spoke about thee. He said to them: You have dismissed the Living One before you and you have spoken about the dead.'

[5] Cp. Gärtner, pp. 45 f.

[6] It is noteworthy, however, that Quispel has noted here four agreements with the Diatessaron against Matthew (*VigChr* XIII, 1959, pp. 113 f.).

follows: (i) He omits to mention that the farmer sowed seed in his field. (ii) He omits to record that the corn grew before it was noticed that darnel had been sown among the wheat. (iii) In Thomas the conversation between the farmer and his labourers is abbreviated and less vivid than in Matthew. (iv) The vital words 'Let both grow together until the harvest' are omitted in Thomas's version. (v) In Thomas there is no mention of the darnel being bound into bundles to be burned. Thus the main point of the original story has been lost; for, according to B. T. D. Smith, the farmer intended to turn his enemies' stratagem to his own profit by using the darnel as firewood.[1]

On the whole Thomas's versions of the parables are inferior to those of the Synoptic Gospels inasmuch as Thomas's additional material can usually be recognized as embellishments and his shorter versions seem more likely to be the result of compression. In a few cases, however, Thomas provides a text which may be more original than that of the Synoptic Gospels.

2. CHANGE OF AUDIENCE

Jeremias has suggested that a very large number of Jesus' parables were originally addressed to his opponents or to the crowd, and that the needs of the early Church for material to be used by church members tended to result in a change of the audience to whom the parables were addressed, and a consequent change in the meaning of such parables.[2]

There are some synoptic parables which are addressed in one Gospel to the disciples and in other Gospels to the crowd or to Jesus' opponents. In each case where these parables find a parallel in Thomas they are addressed there to the disciples, and it is highly probable that Thomas intends them to have a gnostic interpretation. Thus the Parable of the Mustard Seed is addressed to the crowd in Luke 13.18, but in Mark 4.30 and Matt. 13.31 to the disciples. In Thomas 84.28 it is addressed to the disciples.[3] The meaning probably here is that the Mustard Seed is the true

---

[1] *Op. cit.*, p. 198.

[2] *Op. cit.*, p. 31.

[3] L. Cerfaux (*Muséon* LXX, pp. 311 f.) thinks that Thomas's Parable of the Mustard Seed is dependent upon Mark's version; but his argument is slender.

gnosis.[1] Further details of Thomas's parable confirm this interpretation. For the mustard seed only grows when it falls on the 'tilled earth' (84.31), i.e. when it finds a home in the well-prepared soul of the gnostic believer.[2]

There is a further group of parables and similitudes which in the Synoptic Gospels are addressed only to Jesus' opponents or to the multitude, but which in Thomas's version are addressed to Jesus' disciples. The change of audience has in every case resulted in a change of meaning. Thus the Parable of the Sower is intended by Thomas to represent the growth of true gnosis.[3] This interpretation is confirmed by the statement in Thomas that the seed which fell on the rock and did not strike root 'sent no ear up to heaven' (82.8). This seems to be a reference to the heavenward ascent of the soul of the true gnostic.

A further example is furnished by the Parable of the Banquet (92.10 ff.). Thomas intends his readers to understand from this parable that commerce is incompatible with the contemplation required of the true gnostic. The details of the parable have been altered to give the story this meaning. The excuses offered by those who do not accept an invitation to the banquet are all concerned with commerce, and this is the only one of Thomas's parables which has a generalizing conclusion: 'Tradesmen and merchants (shall) not (enter) the places of my Father' (92.34 f.).

---

[1] Doresse (p. 152) cites Hipp. *Ref.* 5.9.6, where the beliefs of Naassenes are recounted. He speaks of 'a point which is nothing, which is composed of nothing because it has no parts, and which will develop by its own efforts an inalienable grandeur. This point is the Kingdom of Heaven, the grain of mustard seed, the indivisible point which exists in the body, the point which no one knows except only the gnostics.'

[2] Other examples of such parables are: (i) The Parable of the Light (Luke 11.34 f. to the crowd; Matt. 6.22 f. and Thomas 86.6 to the disciples); (ii) The Parable of the Lampstand (Luke 11.33 ff. to the crowd; Mark 4.21 f., Matt. 5.15 f., Luke 8.16 f., and Thomas 87.13 to the disciples); (iii) The Parable of the Grapes and Thistles (Matt. 12.33 f. to Jesus' opponents; Matt. 7.16, Luke 6.44 and Thomas 88.31 to the disciples); (iv) The Parable of the Treasure in the Heart (Matt. 12.35 f. to Jesus' opponents; Luke 6.45 f. and Thomas 88.34 to Jesus' disciples); (v) The Parable of the Leaven (Luke 13.20 f. to the crowd; Matt. 13.33 ff. and Thomas 97.2 to the disciples); (vi) The Parable of the Lost Sheep (Luke 15.4 ff. to the crowd; Matt. 18.12 ff. and Thomas 98.22 to the disciples).

[3] Doresse (p. 136) cites a passage from Hippolytus (*Ref.* 5.8.30) according to which the gnostics interpreted the Parable of the Sower thus: 'That signifies the mysteries which only the perfect gnostics have heard.'

A third example is given by Thomas's version of the Parable of the Vineyard (93.1 ff.). In the synoptic versions the parable is addressed either to Jesus' opponents (Mark 12.1; Matt. 21.33) or to the crowd (Luke 20.9). In Thomas's version, which is addressed to the disciples, the point of the parable does not concern Jesus but the true gnosis. This is made plain by the ensuing saying. Whereas the Synoptic Gospels follow up the parable by Jesus' citation of Ps. 118.22 and by his interpretation of this *testimonium* as pointing to himself, Thomas 93.17 f. uses it in a different way. 'Jesus said: Show me the stone which the builders rejected.' Jesus himself is not the stone: the next saying makes it evident that the stone is the self-knowledge of the true gnostic: 'Jesus said: Whoever knows the All but fails (to know) himself lacks everything' (93.19 f.).[1]

In fact, the only people who converse with Jesus in Thomas are 'the disciples', and in particular Thomas,[2] Simon Peter,[3] Matthew,[4] Mary[5] and Salome.[6] The only occasion when Jesus is addressed by anyone outside this circle is when 'a woman of the multitude said to him: Blessed is the womb that bore thee and the breasts which nourished thee' (95.3 ff.). The Gospel according to Thomas was evidently written for a closed circle of gnostic Christians, so that we should expect to see parables, which were originally addressed to Jesus' enemies and opponents and to the multitudes, given a new meaning for gnostic readers.

3. THE HORTATORY USE OF PARABLES BY THE CHURCH

Jeremias has suggested that, while the parables in the mouth of Jesus usually referred to the eschatological crisis which Jesus'

[1] Other examples of a change of audience and a consequent change of meaning are: (i) The Parable of the Strong Man (87.20 ff.) which here refers to Jesus' conquest of 'the world'; (ii) The Parable of the Wineskins (89.17 ff.) which refers to the gnostic's life in the new world; (iii) The Parable of the Patch (89.22 f.) which has the same meaning; (iv) The Parable of the Rich Fool (92.2 ff.) which refers to the dangers of commercial success; (v) The Parable of the Foxes and Birds (95.34 ff.) which refers to the true 'rest' of the gnostic; (vi) The Parable of the Signs of the Sky (96.22 ff.) which refers to the ignorance of those who do not possess true gnosis.
[2] 83.2–8.
[3] 82.32 f.; 99.18 f.
[4] 82.34.
[5] 84.34 f.
[6] 91.30 f.

ministry was bringing, the early Church, when this crisis of the ministry had passed, tended to use such parables for hortatory purposes within the Christian community.[1]

The Gospel according to Thomas, however, is remarkable for its absence of hortatory material. Sayings of Jesus which have a direct bearing on conduct are notable for their absence in Thomas. It follows that parables are not used in this sayings collection for hortatory purposes.[2] On the contrary, they are all used in order to show the true way of gnosis. The dragnet brings in a large catch of all kinds: all is thrown back into the sea except for the one large fish—the true gnostic (82.2).[3] The seed is sown on all kinds of soil: but only that sown in the soul of the true gnostic rises towards heaven and bears good fruit (82.12). The mustard seed which falls on the 'tilled' soil' of the true gnostic provides real shelter from the hazards of life (84.33). The true believer will be continually on his watch against the world: he will not let the thief get into his house and take away his precious goods (85.9). The true gnostic is a 'light-man' whose radiance shines throughout the world (86.9). Only the true gnostic can see into the condition of others, because he alone has the self-knowledge which gives him clear vision (86.16). He is manifest to all, he alone knows the spiritual meaning of fasting, and he is impregnable, like a strong city built on a high mountain (87.8). His light is not hidden: it shines like a light on a lampstand which illuminates all who pass by (87.16). Those who have not this knowledge are like the blind trying to lead the blind: both come to disaster (87.19). True knowledge is the only means whereby a man may conquer the world, just as a thief overpowers a strong man before he spoils his house (87.23).[4] One who is not a gnostic can no more bear good fruit than a briar can bear grapes (88.31). A man's treasure

---

[1] *Op. cit.*, pp. 31 ff.

[2] The only parable included by Thomas which originally had a hortatory meaning is the Parable of the Mote and the Beam (86.12–17) and this has been given a gnostic interpretation by the redactor.

[3] Quispel (*NTS* V, 1959, p. 288) suggests another interpretation, quoting in support Clem. Alex. *Strom.* 6.11, § 95.3, and *Heliand* 2628. According to this the 'large fish' refers to the true gnosis which the wise man prefers to all else. For a similar interpretation, cf. H. W. Bartsch, *NTS* VI, 1960, p. 259.

[4] Gärtner (p. 183) suggests that the strong man and his house here stand for the body.

lies not in external things, but in the disposition of his heart (89.5). True knowledge is so different from other kinds of knowledge that the one can no more be fittingly combined with the other than a wine can be put into a different wineskin (89.19) or a garment can be patched with material of a different age (89.22). In this world the gnostic must live with others: but on the day of harvest he will be separated from the others as wheat is separated from weeds (91.6). Those who make themselves rich out of commerce may seem to do well in the world, but they cannot escape death (92.9). Commerce causes men to make excuses: tradesmen and merchants will not enter into the places of the Father (92.35). The true gnostic will suffer persecution (93.15); but knowledge is the true cornerstone of life. It is the pearl which is worth all that a man has (94.18). If the gnostic comes to Christ, he will find true repose for his soul (96.19). Only knowledge enables a man to know true reality (96.22). This gnosis is small and hidden, but it produces great results, like leaven in dough (97.5).[1] And so the gnostic is more valuable than anyone else, for he possesses this knowledge: therefore God will love him and care for him like the shepherd who sought out his lost sheep (98.27). True knowledge is as precious as treasure found in a field; and in the heart of a true believer it multiplies itself and increases its influence (99.3).

4. THE INFLUENCE OF THE CHURCH'S SITUATION

(a) The Church in the Hellenistic World

Many of the synoptic parables reflect an agricultural community. It has already been noted that the excuses in Thomas's version of the Parable of the Banquet are all concerned with commerce, a change of emphasis caused by a changed environment (92.10 ff.).[2] In the Lucan version the reasons for not attending the banquet are connected with a field, a yoke of oxen and a marriage (Luke 14.18 ff.). In Matthew no excuses are given, but

[1] Gärtner (p. 231) suggests that the leaven here stands for the heavenly particle of light or the spiritual element in man.
[2] Gärtner (p. 48) points out that 'it was not merely in Jewish circles that commerce was looked upon with suspicion and a word of warning'.

one guest went to his field, and another to his merchandise (Matt. 22.5). It is generally agreed that Matthew here is inferior to Luke. In Thomas four excuses are given: one concerns claims against merchants, another the arranging of a wedding dinner, another the buying of a house, and the fourth the collection of rent from a village which has been bought (92.15–29). Thomas therefore takes Matthew's alterations further in the same direction.

A similar difference of emphasis can be seen in Thomas's version of the Parable of the Rich Fool (92.2–10). According to Luke, a rich farmer's land has prospered: he has such a bumper crop that his storage facilities are insufficient for his needs. The point of Luke's parable is the futility of rich ease (Luke 12.16–21). Thomas's version is subtly different. A rich man decides to grow his own produce so that he may be completely self-sufficient: he therefore invests in agriculture and indulges in what must have been the equivalent of 'expense-account farming'. In Thomas the point of the parable is the futility of attempting material self-sufficiency.

An interesting point arises in connexion with Thomas's version of the Parable of the Lampstand (87.13–17). There are grounds (which will be considered later) for holding that Thomas's version is an early form of the parable derived from a source independent of the Synoptic Gospels. However, it has been suggested that a lampstand placed in the vestibule of a house introduces a Hellenistic note. Jeremias maintains[1] that in the little, windowless, one-roomed peasant houses of Palestine, it may have been customary to place a bushel-measure over the lamp in order to extinguish it (cf. 87.14 and synoptic parallels), since blowing it out might cause an unpleasant smell and might even be dangerous because of sparks. The light when lit would give illumination to *all* the house, and not merely to those who go in (Luke 11.33) or out (Thomas 87.16 f.). If we could be certain that Jesus, in speaking this parable, was referring only to the houses of Jewish *fellahin,* Jeremias's point would be valid. But not all Palestinians dwelt in such humble homes: there must have been many houses on the Hellenistic model, in which a lamp in the vestibule would illuminate 'those going in and out', as Thomas's

[1] *Op. cit.,* pp. 96 f.

version narrates. This may therefore be an authentic detail.

(b) The Gnostic Church

There are many indications in the Gospel of Thomas as a whole that it is a gnostic work, and evidence for this is not lacking in the parables. For example, the Kingdom is compared to a 'wise' merchant (94.17) and to a 'wise' fisherman (81.29, 34); but this epithet is absent in the Matthaean parallels (Matt. 13.45, 47).[1] Words which are associated with gnostic systems of thought appear in some of Thomas's parables. For example, *topos* is found in gnostic teaching,[2] and it obtrudes in several parables. Thus, in the introduction to the Parable of the Light, the disciples say, 'Show us the *topos* where thou art' (86.4). Or again, at the conclusion of the Parable of the Banquet, Thomas has: 'Tradesmen and merchants shall not enter the *topos* of my Father' (92.35).[3] Similarly, Repose, *anapausis*, plays a part in the gnostic thought of Thomas[4] (cf. 90.7, 8; 91.21; 96.19), and the 'light-man' (86.7) appears elsewhere in gnostic teaching.[5]

One aspect of gnosticism lies in its emphasis on the individual. Many parables have been slightly altered so as to bring out this teaching about individuals. A good example is furnished by the Parable of the Banquet. In Matthew and Luke there are no invitations to individuals, only individual excuses. The guests are summoned with the message that 'all things are ready' (Luke 14.17; cf. Matt. 22.4). According to Thomas, however, the servant says to each guest: 'My master summons thee' (92.14, 19, 22, 26). In the Synoptic Gospels the emphasis is on the work of God in preparing the feast: in Thomas upon the individual invitations.

The Parable of the Lost Sheep emphasizes a similar point. According to Matthew, the shepherd rejoices over the lost sheep which he has found (Matt. 18.13). According to Luke, he summons his friends and neighbours to share his joy with them (Luke 15.6). But according to Thomas the shepherd speaks to

---

[1] Cf. Thomas 83.1; 85.16.

[2] Doresse (p. 162) cites Hippolytus, *Ref.* 8.10.9, as an illustration of the way in which the gnostic sectaries conceived of 'the eternal places'.

[3] Cf. Thomas 81.8; 91.21; 93.23.

[4] Grant/Freedman (p. 152) refer to the Naassene speculations about rest and movement reported by Hippolytus (*Ref.* 5.7.25).

[5] The concept of the 'light-man' appears in *Pistis Sophia* 125.

the lost sheep itself (98.27).[1] Moreover, according to Thomas, the sheep which went astray was the largest[2] of the flock (98.24). This is presumably an allegorizing detail,[3] and the reader is intended to understand that the gnostic believer is the most important class of Christian, for he alone possesses true spiritual knowledge.[4]

Presumably the same kind of individualism has influenced Thomas's version of the Similitude of the Yoke (96.16–19). In Matthew the invitation is addressed to the burdened and heavy laden (Matt. 11.28), while in Thomas the invitation is general and the addressees are not specified: presumably it will be accepted only by the true gnostic. In Matthew the invitation is to learn from Jesus and to receive at his hands rest for the soul. In Thomas the disciples are told that they will find rest for themselves, and there is no mention of learning from Jesus. It is significant that Matthew mentions 'burden' twice: Thomas not at all. Presumably the gnostic does not have burdens which need relief.

Thomas's phrase 'Kingdom of the Father' emphasizes the same individualism.[5] Thus in Matt. 13.45 we read: 'The Kingdom of Heaven is like to a merchant . . .' But Thomas's version is as follows: 'The Kingdom of the Father is like a merchant . . .'

---

[1] According to Thomas, the shepherd says: 'I love thee more than the ninety-nine.' Guillaumont (*Journal Asiatique* CCXLVI, p. 120) has pointed out that the same Aramaic word can be translated 'love' (as in Thomas) or 'rejoice over' (as in Matt. 18.13).

[2] Cf. the 'large fish' (82.1); the 'large branch' (84.32).

[3] H. W. Bartsch (*NTS* VI, p. 255), however, regards it as a mere explanatory expansion. Gärtner, however, suggests that 'large' stands for the heavenly element (p. 231).

[4] In the Gospel of Truth the parable appears thus: 'He is the Shepherd who left the ninety and nine sheep which had not gone astray; he rejoiced when he found it. For ninety and nine is a number which is counted on the left hand, which comprehends it, but when the one is found the total number passes to the right hand' (*Evangelium Veritatis*, ed. M. Malinine, H. Ch. Puech, G. Quispel [Zurich, 1956], pp. 31 f.). A complex and cognate system of numerology was, according to Irenaeus (*Adv. haer.* 1.16.2), in vogue among the Valentinians. Gärtner (pp. 235 f.) suggests that in Thomas's version the ninety-nine sheep represent the heavenly world, while the lost sheep stands for that part of the light-world which is imprisoned in the material universe.

[5] Cf. L. Cerfaux, *Muséon* LXX, pp. 316 ff. For variations in Thomas's usage, cf. Gärtner, pp. 211 f.

(94.14). The same change can be seen in the Parable of the Leaven (97.3: cf. Matt. 13.33; Luke 13.30), and in the Parable of the Wheat and Tares (90.33: cf. Matt. 13.24). 'The Kingdom of the Father' is also used in two parables which are not found elsewhere (97.7, 15), as well as in a logion which has parallels in the Synoptic Gospels (97.26: cf. Mark 3.35; Matt. 12.50; Luke 8.21).[1]

According to gnostic thought, the Kingdom of Heaven is not a future eschatological event involving the community, but a state of being which is achieved when the individual is enlightened with true knowledge. It is a present reality rather than a future event. This difference in outlook influences some of Thomas's parables and similitudes.[2] Thus, in Thomas's version, if a blind man leads a blind man, both fall into a pit (87.18 ff.), while according to the synoptics, they *will* both fall into a pit (Matt. 15.14; Luke 6.39). The Parable of the Thief instances a similar change.[3] Thomas has here a different interpretation from that of the Synoptic Gospels. According to Thomas, this parable is a warning to 'watch for the world' (85.11; cf. 98.7), while the context of this parable in the canonical Gospels shows it to be concerned with the Parousia (Mark 13.35 f.; Matt. 24.43 f.; Luke 12.39 f.). Again, in the Similitude of the Signs of the Times, the point of the saying in the Synoptic Gospels is that Jesus' hearers cannot discern the present crisis (Luke 12.56; cf. Matt. 16.3). In Thomas, however, Jesus' hearers are unable to discern the present crisis because of their lack of knowledge: 'Him who is before your face you have not known' (96.23 f.).

5. ALLEGORIZATION

It is generally agreed that there was a tendency in the early Church to interpret the parables of Jesus allegorically and that this tendency has left its mark on the synoptic material; although there is disagreement among scholars about the amount of allegorization which was due to the early Church, and how much was already present in the teaching of Jesus. Some of the allegorical interpretations of Gospel parables, however, must be secondary.

[1] Cf. also Thomas 99.16 and Luke 17.20.
[2] Cf. Gärtner, p. 70.
[3] Cf. Gärtner, p. 178.

For example, the explanation of the Parable of the Sower (Mark 4.13–20; Matt. 13.18–23; Luke 8.11–15) must be attributed to the early Church on linguistic grounds alone.[1] It is very striking that Thomas simply records the parable without providing any explanation, allegorical or otherwise (82.3–13). Similarly, the explanation of the Parable of the Wheat and Tares in Matthew must be attributed to Matthew himself [2] (Matt. 13.36–43). Once again, Thomas simply records the parable without any allegorical explanation (90.33–91.7).

Thomas does not merely fail to include allegorical explanations of parables where they are appended to these parables in the Synoptic Gospels. Some of Thomas's parables themselves, which have their counterpart in the Synoptic Gospels, do not include details which are evidently intended by the synoptic evangelists to be understood allegorically. The Parable of the Banquet is a conspicuous example of this lack of allegorizing detail (Thomas 92.10–35; Matt. 22.1–11; Luke 14.16–24). Matthew records a story about a king (God) who makes a marriage feast for his son (Jesus). He reports the anger of the king and the destruction wrought by his armies (the destruction of Jerusalem in AD 70). Luke, on the other hand, although he does not include these allegorizing details, does add a second mission of the man's servant to compel those found in the highways and hedges to come in, an evident reference to the Gentile mission of the Church. Thomas, however, has none of these allegorizing details. Luke's Parable of the Banquet is generally agreed to be more primitive than Matthew's Parable of the Wedding Breakfast, and Thomas has more affinities with Luke's parable than with Matthew's: (i) In Matthew the King dispatches 'servants' (22.3) and then 'other servants' (v. 4). In Thomas, as in Luke, only one servant is dispatched (92.12; Luke 14.17). (ii) Matthew does not record the words of the guests, but both Luke and Thomas report the vivid words of those who would not come: 'I pray to be excused' (Luke 14.18, 19; 92.16, 25, 28). (iii) According to Matthew the feast is given by a king (22.2), according to Luke (14.16), and Thomas (92.10) by 'a man'.[3] Luke's and Thomas's

[1] Cf. Jeremias, *op. cit.*, p. 61.

[2] *Ibid.*, pp. 64 ff.

[3] Synoptic parables sometimes begin with this or a similar expression. Cf. Luke 10.30.

greater simplicity here seems preferable. In two respects Thomas's version of the parable seems to be superior to Luke: (i) Thomas omits the allegorizing detail about the Gentile mission mentioned above. (ii) Thomas records that the man sent out his servant and told him 'to go out to the roads: bring those whom thou shalt find, so that they may dine' (92.32 ff.). This resembles Matthew, who has 'call as many as you shall find to the marriage' (22.9). Luke, however, has an invitation to the poor, lame, blind and maimed (14.21). It is difficult to believe that Luke's version here is better than Thomas's, for all his categories of invited guests correspond to the kind of folk whom Jesus healed.

A further example of Thomas's lack of allegorizing detail is provided by the Parable of the Wicked Husbandmen (93.1–16). (i) It has already been noted that Thomas omits to explain that the owner of the vineyard was an absentee landlord. But perhaps the prominence of this detail in the Synoptic Gospels (Mark 12.1; Matt. 21.33; Luke 20.9) is due to its allegorical interpretation: the absentee owner represents the invisible God. (ii) In the Synoptic Gospels it is recorded that the owner of the vineyard sent his emissary at the due time (*kairos*) (Mark 12.2 *et par.*). This detail is omitted in Thomas. Possibly *kairos* was understood allegorically by the synoptic evangelists as the moment of salvation, and for this reason the word may have been added to the story by Mark (or by his source). (iii) According to Mark, first one servant is dispatched to the labourers (12.2), then another (v. 4), then a third (v.5) and then many others (*ibid.*). Matthew records first the dispatch of one group of three servants who were respectively beaten, killed and stoned (21.35); and then a second and larger group of servants who suffered the same fate (v. 36). Luke narrates the dispatch of one servant who was beaten (20.10), then a second who suffered the same fate (v. 11), and then a third who returned wounded (v. 12). According to Thomas, however, only two servants were sent before the son of the owner was dispatched, and they were both beaten (93.6–11). Matthew's two groups of servants may well represent the former and the latter prophets. Mark's 'many others' seems to be an allegorizing detail referring in general to the persecution of the prophets by the Jewish people. Luke's narrative seems free here from allegory, but Thomas's is to be preferred, for by his record of only two servants dispatched before the son was sent he retains the much-used Jewish triplet.[1] (iv) Certain expressions used in the Synoptic Gospels about the treatment which the emissaries received at the hands of the farm-labourers suggest that an allegorical interpretation is intended: they were 'killed, stoned, beheaded, wounded, shamefully treated, cast out'. According to Thomas they were merely beaten 'and a little longer and they would have been killed'. Thomas here seems likely to be the most original version, because it is the simplest. (v) All the synoptic versions record that the owner sent last of all his 'only son'. The word ἀγαπητόν may well be an allegorical detail, a Christological addition. The word does not appear in Thomas's version. (vi) In Mark the son is killed and his body is thrown out of the vineyard (Mark 12.8). According to Matthew and Luke the son was first cast out of the vineyard and then killed (Matt. 21.39; Luke 20.15), and this small alteration is presumably due to Jesus' death 'without the camp' (cf. Heb. 13.12). In Thomas the story reads very simply: 'they seized him, they slew him' (93.15). Thomas's simplicity is to be preferred.[2]

It is not impossible that Thomas used the Synoptic Gospels as his sources, and that he has emended and compressed the synoptic versions of these two parables so that the allegorical interpretations imposed on them by the early Church or the canonical evangelists have been excised, in order that the resulting stories could have a new (gnostic) interpretation read into them. (Thomas could have done this the more easily if he were merely reproducing synoptic material from memory, but the existence of doublets makes this hypothesis extremely improbable.) But it is hard to resist the conclusion that Thomas has been using an independent and in some ways a more primitive source for these parables. This does not mean that the whole of Thomas's versions of these parables are superior to those of the Synoptic Gospels: on the contrary, it has already been pointed out that they are in many respects greatly inferior. But it does mean that

[1] Cf. R. McL. Wilson, 'Thomas and the Synoptic Gospels', *ExpT* LXXII, 1960, p. 37.

[2] R. M. Grant, however, concludes from a comparative study of Thomas and the Synoptic Gospels here that the former's procedure 'proves that Thomas relies on the Synoptic Gospels' ('Notes on the Gospel of Thomas', *VigChr* XIII, 1959, p. 178).

Thomas was using a source which had not suffered the addition of the allegorizing details which are found in the Synoptic Gospels and which is in that respect superior and more primitive.

Thomas's use of the formula 'He who has ears to hear, let him hear' suggests that he intended an esoteric meaning to be read into his parables.[1] When this formula appears in the Synoptic Gospels it usually implies that the words which precede or follow them signify more than their surface meaning.[2] Thomas uses the formula more frequently than the synoptic evangelists, and always before or after a parable or figurative saying.[3] Probably the reason why no allegorical details are included in Thomas's text, and no allegorical explanations are appended to Thomas's parables is to be found in the desire to keep the 'true' spiritual interpretation of the sayings hidden from all except gnostic initiates. It is probably on this account that Thomas leaves some of his parables in a comparatively primitive state, while he seems to be prepared to alter many of Jesus' sayings drastically to suit his gnostic purpose.

6. COLLECTION AND CONFLATION OF PARABLES

(a) Double Parables

A few parables which are found paired in one or more of the Synoptic Gospels appear in Thomas similarly paired. Thus the Parables of the Patches and Wineskins (Mark 2.21 f.; Matt. 9.16 f.; Luke 5.36–38) are also paired in Thomas (89.17–23). But whereas in the Synoptic Gospels the Parable of the Patch precedes that of the Wine, in Thomas it follows it. There is no reason why Thomas should have inverted this order if he was following a synoptic source. But his procedure becomes comprehensible if he was following an independent tradition which had already inverted

---

[1] Cf. Iren., *Adv. haer.* 1.3.1 f.: 'They tell us that this knowledge is not openly proclaimed because not all are able to understand it, but that it is secretly revealed by the Saviour through parables to such as can understand it.'

[2] Mark 4.9, 23; 7.16 ; Matt. 11.15; 13.9, 43; Luke 8.8; 14.35.

[3] 82.2; 85.19; 86.6; 92.9; 93.16; 97.6. Wilson points out that the phrase is used four times in the Matthaean form and twice in that of Mark and Luke (*Studies*, pp. 52 f.).

the order—this could easily have happened in oral tradition before the parables were set down in writing. As for the Parable of the Patch, the case has been argued above for Luke's version being a conflation of Mark with Thomas's source (Luke 5.36; Mark 2.21; Thomas 89.22 f.). As for the Parable of the Wineskins, Thomas is nearer to Luke than he is to Mark 2.22 or Matt. 9.17. For Luke has a sentence not found in the other Synoptic Gospels: 'And no one having drunk new wine, desires new. For he says, The old is good' (Luke 5.39). Thomas has: 'No man drinks old wine and immediately desires to drink new wine' (89.17 f.). But Thomas includes a sentence not found elsewhere: 'And they do not put old wine into a new wineskin, lest it spoil it' (89.20 ff.). According to the parallelism of Hebrew poetry (new wine/old wineskins: old wine/new wineskins) Thomas's version is to be preferred. Here, then, is an additional reason for the view that Thomas here uses a source independent of the Synoptic Gospels.

Another pair of parables in the Synoptic Gospels consists of sayings about two kinds of tree and two kinds of treasure (Matt. 12.33 ff.; Luke 6.43 ff.; cf. Matt. 7.16 ff.). Thomas has a similar pair of parables (88.31–89.5), and his version is closer to Luke than to the Matthaean doublets, although he omits the logion about the good and bad tree which is found in the synoptics. Thomas, however, has four differences from Luke: (i) Thomas has the same order as Matthew: 'grapes: thorns' and 'figs: thistles' (88.31 ff.; contrast Luke 6.44b). (ii) Thomas has the phrase 'the evil treasure which is in his heart' (89.3). This is a Semitism and is found in the *Heliand*: this suggests that Tatian followed this peculiar reading, possibly taking it from the Gospel to the Hebrews.[1] (iii) Thomas adds to the sentence 'an evil man brings forth evil things out of his evil treasure which is in his heart' the additional phrase 'and speaks evil things' (89.4). This addition is also paralleled in various Diatessarons, which seems to suggest that Tatian was following the same tradition as Thomas in this saying.[2] (iv) Thomas has the phrase 'for out of the abundance of the heart he brings forth evil things' (89.5) where Matthew and Luke have 'out of the abundance of the heart (his) mouth speaks'

[1] Quispel (*NTS* V, 1959, p. 286) cites *Heliand* 1775.
[2] Cf. Quispel, *ibid.*

(Matt. 12.34; Luke 6.45); again a different tradition.[1] Quispel
comments on this saying: 'More than once we find a saying meets
all the conditions we stipulated: it shows traces of having been
translated from the Aramaic, it can be paralleled in Jewish Christian sources, and it has its echo in the Diatessaron and the Western
Text. Then I am practically sure it is of Jewish Christian origin.'[2]

Of the other paired parables in the Synoptic Gospels, none of
them appear in Thomas in pairs. This is not surprising, since it
can be shown that the pairing in these cases does not go back
beyond Mark, Matthew or Luke. For the Parable of the Lamp,
which is paired in Mark 4.21 ff. with the Parable of the Measure,
is found without it in Luke 11.33 and Matt. 5.15 as well as in
Thomas 87.13 f.; and the Parable of the Lost Sheep, which is
paired with the Parable of the Lost Coin in Luke 15.4–8, is transmitted independently in Matt. 18.12–14 as well as in Thomas
98.22–27. Similarly the Parable of the Mustard Seed, which is
paired with the Parable of the Leaven in Matt. 13.31–33 and Luke
13.18–21, is found by itself in Mark 4.30–32 as well as in Thomas
84.28–33.

The Parables of the Treasure and the Pearl are found paired in
Matt. 13.44–47, and they are not found elsewhere in the Synoptic
Gospels. They can, however, be paralleled in Thomas, but they
are not paired there (98.31–99.3; 94.14–18). It is very probable
that Thomas has taken these from a source independent of Matthew for the following reasons: (i) If Thomas took them from
Matthew, it is impossible to account satisfactorily for their
separation in his sayings collection. (ii) The Parable of the
Treasure in Thomas is so different from the Matthaean version
that it is difficult to see how the former was derived from the
latter. (iii) In Thomas's version of the Parable of the Pearl, it is
reported that the merchant was prudent: in Matthew there is no
mention of this. However, Thomas's reading can be paralleled in

[1] Quispel points out (*VigChr* XI, 1957, p. 198) that Codex Palatinus on
Luke 6.45 supports Thomas here.
[2] *Ibid.* R. M. Grant (*VigChr* XIII, p. 177) adduces the Naassene practice
of linking together synoptic logia to form gnostic *catenae*, and dismisses the
passage in question as constructed out of synoptic sayings. H. W. Bartsch
(*NTS* VI, pp. 253 f.) concurs. Gärtner (pp. 37 ff.) cites Iren., *Adv. haer.*
1.8.1, for the gnostic attempts 'to twist ropes out of sand' by altering the
order and connexion of dominical sayings, especially in the parables. Gärtner
sees this tendency at work here and elsewhere in Thomas.

an early Jewish Christian writing.[1] It seems therefore that Thomas derives his story from a different tradition. Other details of Thomas's parable differ from Matthew's: in Thomas the person concerned was a general merchant with an eye for a bargain: in Matthew he was specifically looking for pearls. (iv) Although Thomas separates the Parables of the Pearl and the Treasure, he follows the Parable of the Pearl with a logion about treasure. It has been suggested that Thomas adds this saying because of Matthew's pairing of the two parables.[2] If this is so, it probably means that Thomas is directly dependent upon Matthew. But it is exceedingly improbable. In the first case the Parable of the Treasure is placed *before* the Parable of the Pearl in Matthew, while in Thomas a saying about treasure is placed *after* the Parable of the Pearl. Secondly, Thomas adds the logion about treasure in order to give an interpretation to the Parable of the Pearl. What is the Pearl? What does it represent to Thomas? It is 'the treasure which fails not, which endures, there where no moth comes near to devour and where no worm destroys' (94.20 ff.). In other words it is the world of the spirit contrasted with the material world of the body which worms can devour.

Matthew also pairs the Parable of the City on a Hill with the Parable of the Lampstand (5.14b–15). Thomas separates these two parables by a single logion about preaching from a housetop (87.10–12) which can be paralleled in a Q saying (Matt. 10.27: Luke 12.3). Thomas has probably inserted this saying between the two parables, for it fits in well with the theme: in fact, it fits in better here than in its synoptic contexts, and it is just possible that Thomas preserves here the original place for this logion.[3] The juxtaposition of the two Parables of the City on a Hill and the Lampstand in Thomas (87.8–17) does not mean that Thomas is dependent here on Matthew, for probably these two

---

[1] Quispel (*VigChr* XII, 1958, p. 191) cites Clem. *Recog.* 3.62: *solum prudentem.*

[2] Grant/Freedman, p. 167.

[3] Grant/Freedman suggest (pp. 94 f.) that Thomas placed this saying here because the word 'light' appears in the synoptic parallels (Matt. 10.27; Luke 12.3). This suggestion assumes that Thomas built up this section from the Synoptic Gospels. It is interesting that Hippolytus, describing Naassene syncretism, writes of 'light not under a bushel but on a candlestick, proclaiming its message on the housetops' (*Ref.* 5.7.28).

parables were paired in very early tradition and possibly even in the teaching of Jesus. There are grounds for holding that Thomas derives his version of these two parables from a source independent of the Synoptic Gospels. The saying about a City set on a Hill is found in a slightly different version in the Oxyrhynchus papyrus: 'A town built on the summit of a high mountain and fortified cannot fall or be concealed.'[1] The Coptic version reads: 'A city which is being built on a high mountain (and) fortified cannot fall nor will it be able to be hid' (87.8 f.). Thus Thomas's version certainly goes back to the second century. Vaganay had independently come to the conclusion that the Oxyrhynchus fragment comes from a source different from the Synoptic Gospels.[2] Further support for Thomas can be found in the third Clementine Homily (which has 'a high mountain' instead of the Matthaean 'mountain' and 'built' instead of 'situated').[3] Furthermore, Quispel has pointed out that this variant has the support of the Persian Diatessaron and the *Heliand*.[4] It seems probable, therefore, that Thomas's version goes back to a different Jewish Christian tradition of the saying. Indeed, this tradition seems preferable to that of the Synoptic Gospels, for it retains both a Semitic form of poetic parallelism[5] and Old Testament allusions[6] which Hoskyns and Davey demonstrated to be a frequent parabolic characteristic.[7] Grant and Freedman's objection to Thomas's tradition here seems trivial: namely, that it simply is not true that a fortified city cannot fall.[8] The parable may have originally asserted that fortified cities do not fall; a present tense of custom rather than an absolute generalization.

As for the Parable of the Lampstand, Thomas's version has more affinities with the Lucan version than with Matthew's. The only divergencies from Luke 11.33 are (i) the transposition of 'hidden place' and 'bushel', a trivial difference (87.14 f.; Luke

[1] Pap. Oxy. 1, Saying 6.
[2] *Le Problème Synoptique* (Paris, 1954), pp. 340–3, cited by Quispel (*VigChr* XII, 1959, p. 187).
[3] Quispel, *ibid.*, cites Ps.-Clem. *Hom.* 3.37.
[4] Quispel, *NTS* V, 1959, p. 285.
[5] Cf. C. F. Burney, *The Poetry of Our Lord*, 1925, pp. 63 ff.
[6] Isa. 2.2; 28.4; Jer. 37.18.
[7] Cf. *The Riddle of the New Testament*, 1958 edn., p. 134.
[8] Grant/Freedman, p. 142. Both Grant/Freedman and Fitzmyer (*Theol. Studies* XX, p. 542) believe that Thomas is here based on Matthew.

11.33); and (ii) the addition of 'those who go out' (87.17) to Luke's 'those who come in' who will see the light upon the lampstand. Here Thomas's version is to be preferred to Luke's, for the former preserves the Semitism 'those who come in and go out'.[1] It is noteworthy that, while Thomas is in close agreement with Luke 11.33, he uses a different version from the doublet in Luke 8.16 (which closely follows Mark 4.21). Since Luke 8.16 is addressed to the disciples and Luke 11.33 is addressed to the crowd, it is probable, as Jeremias suggests,[2] that the latter preserves the original audience and therefore probably also the original contents. Thus Thomas prefers to use a saying which is in close agreement with the earliest form of the saying in the Synoptic Gospels.

The argument can be extended a further and most important step. Thomas's saying is different from Matthew's version (5.15) and similar to Luke's (11.33). However, Thomas follows Matthew's order, not Luke's. For in Thomas, as in Matthew, the Parable of the Lampstand follows after the Parable of the City on a Hill, while Luke has a very different context for it in 11.33. It is impossible to believe that Thomas had Matthew and Luke in front of him and decided to follow Matthew's order with one slight modification, but preferred the Lucan doublet of the Parable of the Lampstand in Luke 11.33. Such literary procedure might belong to the twentieth century, but not to the second century. It has already been shown that it is extremely improbable that Thomas is citing the Synoptic Gospels from memory. There remains only one other possible hypothesis. Thomas was following a source different from Matthew, Mark or Luke, and produced from this source his two parables of the City on a Hill and the Lampstand. Matthew had access to a source containing a different version of the Parable of the City on a Hill which he utilized in Matt. 5.14b. Luke, on the other hand, preserves more faithfully than Matthew the Q form of the Parable of the Lampstand (Luke 11.33; Matt. 5.15), while he also includes a doublet of the saying (Luke 8.16) which he takes from Mark 4.21. Thomas preserves an earlier tradition in his version of both the Parable of the City on a Hill and the Parable of the Lampstand.

[1] Cf. Quispel, *NTS* V, 1959, p. 285.
[2] *Parables*, p. 30.

(b) Collection of Parables

'The primitive Church had begun at an early date to make collections of parables.'[1] The collections of parables which can be found in the Synoptic Gospels are not, however, represented in Thomas.[2] In Mark and Matthew the growth of such collections of parables can be noted (Mark 4.3–32; Matt. 13.1–52), but in Thomas these parables are scattered about his sayings collection.[3] The Parable of the Dragnet directly precedes the Parable of the Sower in Thomas (81.28–82.13), while in Matthew the Parable of the Sower precedes the Dragnet, with several parables between them (Matt. 13.1–9; 47–50). The only pair of parables which is found both in Thomas and in one of the Synoptic Gospels has already been discussed: both Matthew and Thomas keep the sequence: City set on a Hill; Lampstand. There is an obvious connexion of thought here, and probably both Matthew and Thomas retain a very early grouping of sayings.

It is noteworthy that Thomas on two occasions groups parables which have their counterpart in the Synoptic Gospels with hitherto unknown parables. In Thomas 84.26–85.6 the Parable of the Mustard Seed precedes the Parable of the Children in the Field. Again, in Thomas 97.2–20, the Parable of the Leaven precedes the two hitherto unknown Parables of the Jar and of the Sword. Probably both these new parables are based upon authentic tradition.[4] The Parable of the Children in the Field, however, has been obviously altered in transmission so that it now carries a gnostic interpretation. Elsewhere in Thomas the theme of innocent nakedness appears (cf. 87.29 ff.), and it is a theme found in other gnostic sayings.[5] It probably refers to death as a stripping off of the body (contrast II Cor. 5.4). The disciples are like 'little children who have installed themselves in a field

---

[1] Jeremias, *op. cit.*, p. 72.

[2] In Thomas 92.1–93.16 can perhaps be seen the beginnings of a new collection. The Parables of the Rich Fool and the Banquet are here placed together because both give a warning about the dangers of materialism. Cf. R. McL. Wilson, *Studies*, p. 90.

[3] Wilson notes that all the parables in Matt. 13 appear in Thomas, but not in the same order or grouping (pp. 53 f.).

[4] Wilson regards these two parables as 'probably the product of later reflection', but he gives no firm grounds for this judgment (*op. cit.*, p. 97).

[5] Clement, *Strom.* 3.13, § 92.2; Hippolytus, *Ref.* 5.8.44.

which is not theirs' inasmuch as they live in the material world.[1] What the original form of the parable was it is now impossible to say. The Parable of the Jar (97.7–14), on the other hand, does not seem to have been so changed in transmission. The point of the story is the woman's imperceptible loss of meal from a broken jar: this probably referred originally to the imperceptible coming of the Kingdom until it has suddenly been seen to have arrived (cf. Mark 4.26 ff.). This was probably originally an authentic parable. It is as homely as the Parable of the Leaven[2] and it is very difficult to imagine the gnostics having made up a parable the subject of which was a woman![3] Thomas's text seems to retain the Semitic asyndeton (lines 10, 11, 12). The ensuing Parable of the Sword (97.15–20) also seems to be authentic, and it does not seem to have been altered in transmission. The point of the parable is that whoever would enter the Kingdom must first reckon up the cost (cf. Luke 14.28 ff., 31 ff.). In the same way a man who intends to commit a murder should first test out his sword on a wall to see that he is strong enough to use it effectively.[4]

If these three fresh parables are based on primitive tradition, it is extremely probable that Thomas also drew from the same source his version of the Parables of the Mustard Seed and the Pearl to which they are attached. This means that Thomas would have drawn his versions of these two parables from a source other than the Synoptic Gospels.

(c) Conflation of Parables

There seem to be only three instances of conflation in Thomas's parables. (i) In his first version of the Parable of the Thief (85.7–14) Thomas records that 'if the lord of the house knows that the thief is coming, he will watch before he comes and will not let him tunnel into his house of his kingdom to carry away his goods. You then watch for the world, gird up your loins with great

[1] For an interpretation of this parable, cf. Gärtner, p. 184.
[2] In the East a woman would be the most likely person to carry a vessel of corn along a road.
[3] Cf. Thomas 99.19 ff.
[4] Swords were commonly worn in Palestine in the first century (cf. Mark 14.47; Luke 22.38).

strength lest the brigands find a way . . .' The phrase 'carry away his goods' seems to come from the Parable of the Strong Man (cf. Thomas 87.22; Mark 3.27;[1] Matt. 12.29), while 'gird up your loins' seems to come from the introduction to the Parable of the Faithful Servants (Luke 12.35).[2] (ii) In Thomas's doublet of the Thief (98.6–10) there seems to be further allusions to Luke's Parable of the Faithful Servants (Luke 12.37 f.).[3] It is not surprising to find these conflations in Thomas's versions, for within the New Testament tradition there has been some confusion. In Mark 13.35 the Parable of the Thief seems to have been almost engulfed by the Parable of the Servants Entrusted with Supervision (Matt. 25.14); while the Thief has been equated with the Son of Man (Matt. 24.44; Luke 12.40), with the Lord (Mark 13.35; Matt. 24.42) and even with the Day of the Lord (I Thess. 5.4). (iii) It is possible that conflation can also be detected in Thomas's version of the Parable of the Treasure Hid in a Field. In Matthew the parable is in more abbreviated state than in Thomas (Matt. 13.44; contrast Thomas 98.31–99.3); for the story in Matthew merely tells how a man was ploughing in a field which did not belong to him and found treasure. Instead of informing the owner of his find, he realized all his assets and bought the field and the treasure with it. In Thomas, however, the point is very different. Both father and son owned a field which contained treasure. Neither knew about the treasure and the son sold the field. Someone bought the field and found the treasure. We are to understand that he realized the treasure for cash, and then 'he lent out the money to whomsoever he wished'. It is possible that Thomas has borrowed some details of his story from a version of the Parable of the Servants Entrusted with Supervision (cf. Matt. 25.14 ff.; Luke 12.42 ff.). But it seems more likely that it has been conflated with a well-known folk-story.[4] This is

[1] Thomas 87.20 reads 'taking by force' the strong man's house; Mark 3.27 'plundering' it. Quispel points out (*NTS* V, 1959, p. 280) that the Aramaic *anas* can bear both meanings.

[2] Grant/Freedman regard this passage as 'a mosaic of sayings chiefly derived from Luke' (p. 135), but H. W. Bartsch believes it comes from tradition independent of the Synoptic Gospels (*NTS* VI, p. 260).

[3] Thomas reads 'Blessed is the man . . .'; cf. Luke 12.37. Thomas further reads 'in which part of the night robbers will come in'; cf. Luke 12.38.

[4] H. W. Bartsch (*op. cit.*, p. 260) fails here to find in Thomas any relation to the synoptic version.

instanced both in Aesop's Fables[1] and in a second-century rabbinic parable.[2] If this is what happened, Thomas provides an adulterated and inferior version.

7. THE SETTING

(a) Contexts created by the Redactor

In the Synoptic Gospels the parables are placed in settings, but inasmuch as in Thomas there is merely a sayings collection, his versions of the parables cannot be said to have proper settings. Nevertheless it is instructive to compare them with the synoptic settings. For example, the synoptic versions of the Parable of the Sower are followed by a saying of Jesus which is thought by Jeremias to be authentic but out of its context: 'To you have been given the mysteries of the kingdom of God, but to those who are outside everything happens in parables' (Mark 4.11 ff.).[3] If Thomas had been following a synoptic source, we should have expected him to include this saying, for it bears a meaning which is consonant with his gnostic tendency. But Thomas does not include this saying. The nearest approach to it is the fragmentary logion in 91.34–92.1: 'I speak my mysteries to those . . . mysteries'; and this can hardly be related to Mark 4.11. The fact that Thomas does not follow the Synoptic Gospels here suggests that he was not following a synoptic source. A similar omission can be seen in connexion with Thomas's version of the Parable of the Yoke (96.16–18). Matthew places before this parable the 'Johannine thunderbolt' (Matt. 11.25–27). It is hard to think of a logion in the Synoptic Gospels more appropriate to Thomas's collection than this; and yet it is not found there. This again suggests that Thomas was following a source different from the Synoptics.

It is interesting to note that Thomas's version of the Parable of the Signs of the Sky is more like the Lucan parallel than the Matthaean text (Matt. 16.2 f.; Luke 12.54 f.). Thomas reads: 'You test the face of the sky and of the earth, and him who is before your face you have not known, and you do not know how

[1] Cf. Grant/Freedman, p. 183.
[2] Cerfaux (*Muséon* CXX, p. 314) cites Simeon ben Jochai *ap. Midr. Cant.* 4.13.
[3] Jeremias, *op. cit.*, pp. 10 ff.

to test this moment' (96.22–25). Luke's text is as follows: 'Hypocrites, you know how to test the face of the earth and the heaven, do you not know how to test this time?' (Luke 12.56). Luke's version here is superior, for Thomas's addition of 'him who is before your face you have not known' spoils the Semitic parallelism, and Thomas's omission of the word 'hypocrites' (Luke 12.56) suggests a change of audience from Jesus' opponents to his disciples, for the disciples are never called hypocrites.[1] Matthew, however, has nothing directly to correspond to this logion, and so Thomas is following the same tradition here as Luke. And yet Thomas sandwiches this parable between two sayings which can be found only in Matthew (Matt. 11.28–30, the Parable of the Yoke; and Matt. 7.6, the saying about not giving what is holy to the dogs). If Thomas was not merely citing synoptic logia from memory (and this hypothesis has already been dismissed) the only satisfactory explanation that can be given of Thomas's procedure is that he was using sources independent of the Synoptic Gospels.

Occasionally Thomas places a parable in a context such that its meaning and point are altered. For example, the Parable of Mote and the Beam is placed in front of a saying about true fasting (86.12–20). By this juxtaposition Thomas means to show that the man who has cast the beam out of his own eye is he who knows the true meaning of fasting. Some such new interpretation of the parable is to be expected, for Thomas gives very little ethical teaching in his collection of sayings, and a parable which originally had an ethical point could be expected to be given a gnostic interpretation.

One further context of Thomas's parables needs to be investigated. Thomas places the Parable of the Banquet in front of the Parable of the Vineyard (92.10–93.16). Luke includes his version of this parable in a collection of sayings about meals (14.7–24). Matthew, however, inserts his version of the Parable of the Banquet into a Marcan context so that it follows after the Parable of the Vineyard (21.33–22.10). If Thomas could be shown to follow Matthew's order, it could be demonstrated that Thomas is dependent on Matthew, since Matthew made his own context for the Parable of the Banquet. However, Thomas does not follow Matthew's order: on the contrary, he places the two parables in

---

[1] For similar omission, cf. Thomas 86.12. Contrast Matt. 7.5; Luke 6.42.

inverse order. Furthermore, Thomas does not add the Parable of the Wedding Garment to the conclusion of his Parable of the Banquet, as Matthew does; and yet it would seem that the former parable would have been well suited to a gnostic interpretation. The lack of this parable in Thomas suggests that he did not find it in his source.

(b) Introductory Formulae

In general, Thomas's introductory formulae betray the hand of the redactor.[1] On thirteen occasions a parable is introduced by the formula 'Jesus said'. In six instances this can be paralleled by a similar introduction in the Synoptic Gospels,[2] but on seven occasions[3] this is an addition which Thomas uses so often elsewhere. On four occasions Thomas begins a parable with the words 'He said'[4] and on another occasion with the words 'Therefore I say'.[5]

On two occasions Thomas introduces the disciples who ask a question of Jesus, and this leads to a parable. Thus Thomas prefaces the Parable of the Mustard Seed with the words: 'The disciples said to Jesus, Tell us what the Kingdom of Heaven is like. He said to them . . .' (84.26 ff.). Again, before the Parable of the Light-man, Thomas has the following introduction: 'His disciples said, Show us the place where thou art, for it is necessary for us to seek it. He said to them . . .' (86.4–6). These requests for secret information are typical of gnostic writings and they must be attributed to the redactor.

Often Thomas introduces his parables with the phrase 'It is like', 'The Kingdom is like', 'The Kingdom of the Father is like'. These introductions correspond to the Aramaic *lᵉ*. With the one exception of the Mustard Seed, the Kingdom is always likened to

---

[1] For similar introductory formulae, cf. W. L. Knox, *Sources of the Synoptic Gospels*, 1953, vol. I, p. 105.

[2] (i) The Sower, 82.3; Mark 4.2; Matt. 13.3; Luke 8.4; (ii) The Tares, 90.33; Matt. 13.24; (iii) The Banquet, 92.10; Matt. 22.1; (iv) The Foxes and Birds, 95.34; Matt. 8.20; Luke 9.58; (v) The Leaven, 97.2; Matt. 13.31; Luke 13.20; (vi) The Lost Sheep, 98.22; Luke 15.4.

[3] (i) The Mote and Beam, 86.12; (ii) The City on a Hill, 87.7; (iii) The Blind, 87.18; (iv) The Strong Man, 87.20; (v) The Grapes and Figs, 88.31; (vi) the Yoke, 96.16; (vii) The Treasure in a Field, 98.31.

[4] (i) The Dragnet, 81.28; (ii) The Mustard Seed, 84.28; (iii) The Vineyard, 93.1; (iv) The Signs of the Sky, 96.22.

[5] The Thief, 85.6.

a person in Thomas. In the Parable of the Tares, the Kingdom is likened to a man who had seed (90.33), as in Matt. 13.24. In the Parable of the Lost Sheep, the Kingdom is like a shepherd (98.22), an introduction that is lacking in synoptic parallels (Matt. 18.12; Luke 15.4). In the Parable of the Pearl the Kingdom of the Father is likened to a man (94.14), just as in Matt. 13.45 the Kingdom of Heaven is likened to a merchant. The remaining three instances are more significant. In the Parable of the Leaven, the Kingdom is likened to the woman who had the leaven (97.3) and not, as in Matt. 13.33, to the leaven itself. Similarly in the Parable of the Treasure in the Field, the Kingdom is likened to a man who had treasure in his field (98.31) and not to the treasure itself, as in Matt. 13.44. Thomas's introduction to his version of the Parable of the Dragnet is strikingly different from its Matthaean parallel. Matthew reads: 'Therefore the Kingdom of Heaven is like unto a net . . .' (13.47), while Thomas begins: 'The Man is like a wise fisherman . . .' (81.29).[1] Thomas's comparison of the Kingdom to persons, rather than to events or things, instances his individualistic conception of the Kingdom. The original Aramaic phrase meant by such an introduction: 'It is the case with . . . as with . . .' But Thomas probably intends his readers to understand that the Kingdom is realized in individuals, for he understands the Kingdom as the spiritual state of the individual gnostic.

(c) The Conclusions of the Parables

Many of the generalizing conclusions of the Synoptic Gospels, although they may themselves be genuine *verba Christi*, have been added by later tradition to the parables in order to give them a meaning and application suited to the situation of the early Church.[2] It is very striking that many of these generalizing conclusions, which did not originally belong to the parables to which they have become attached, are not found in Thomas's versions of the same parables. Thus the Parable of the Dragnet is concluded by Matthew with verses very similar to those with which he ends his explanation of the Parable of the Tares (Matt. 13.49 f.; cf.

[1] Presumably 'Man' represents the true gnostic (cf. Thomas 98.20) but the correct translation may be simply 'a man'.
[2] Cf. Jeremias, *op. cit.*, p. 85.

vv. 41-43).[1] Thomas, however, in his version of these two parables, has no such conclusion. Matthew's emphasis on apocalyptic has often been thought to be responsible for the conclusion
of these parables. Dodd comments on the conclusion of Matthew's
Parable of the Dragnet that it is 'clearly secondary and may be
ignored'.[2] It is possible that Thomas has deliberately excised an
apocalyptic conclusion which he found in his source, for gnostics
had little time for apocalyptic. But it is more probable that
Thomas was using a source which did not include here an
apocalyptic conclusion. A similar omission can be seen in
Thomas's version of the Parable of the Vineyard. He ends with
the enigmatic words 'Whoever has ears, let him hear' (93.16),
while Mark, followed by Matthew and Luke, has: 'What will the
lord of the vineyard do? He will come and will destroy the husbandmen and will give the vineyard to others' (Mark 12.9; cf.
Matt. 21.40 f.; Luke 20.15b f.). The synoptic conclusion rounds
off the allegory, but Thomas's version is not obviously allegorical
in form.

In other instances Thomas also omits the concluding sentence
found in the synoptic parallels. Thus Luke ends the Parable of the
Rich Fool with the words: 'So is he that stores up treasures for
himself and is not rich towards God' (Luke 12.21). Such a conclusion would be appropriate also in Thomas's version; but he
concludes with the words: 'Whoever has ears, let him hear' (92.
9 f.). Again, Thomas has no generalizing conclusion to his version
of the Parable of the Lost Sheep (98.27). Luke, however, ends
with the words: 'For I say unto you that there will be more joy in
heaven over one sinner who repents than over ninety-nine just
persons who need no repentance' (15.7); while Matthew has the
following conclusion: 'So it is not the will of my father who is in
heaven that one of these little ones should perish' (18.14). Although the hypothesis cannot be ruled out that Thomas suppressed
such conclusions in order to keep the meaning of his parables as
esoteric as possible, it seems more probable that he did not include
them because he did not find them in his sources. For he is not altogether averse to adding a sentence at the end of the parable. His

---

[1] Jeremias (*op. cit.*, p. 67) speaks of Matt. 13.49 f. as 'simply a shortened
replica of Matt. 13.40b-43'.
[2] *Parables of the Kingdom*, p. 187.

version of the Parable of the Banquet ends with the words: 'Tradesmen and merchants (shall) not (enter) the places of my Father' (92.34 f.). Thomas has added these words to make them fit in with the meaning which he had given to the parable, and he has been prepared to make considerable changes in the parable itself in order to bring out this meaning.

CONCLUSION

The object of this article has been to compare the parables in Thomas with similar parables in the Synoptic Gospels. In many instances Thomas's versions have proved to be inferior, and such instances of inferiority have usually been connected with Thomas's gnosticizing tendency. Nevertheless it is often the case that Thomas's divergencies from synoptic parallels can be most satisfactorily explained on the assumption that he was using a source distinct from the Synoptic Gospels. Occasionally this source seems to be superior, especially inasmuch as it seems to be free from apocalyptic imagery, allegorical interpretation, and generalizing conclusions. The hypothesis the Thomas did not use the Synoptic Gospels as a source gains strength from a comparative study of the parables' literary affinities together with an examination of the order of sayings and parables in Thomas. It is further confirmed by the attestation of some of Thomas's variants in Jewish Christian tradition. This suggests that Thomas's source may have diverged from the synoptic tradition before the gospel material had been translated from Aramaic into Greek. This in turn suggests that Thomas may have used the Gospel to the Hebrews as the source of many of his parables.

III

THE THEOLOGY OF THE GOSPEL
OF THOMAS

In this chapter we shall be concerned with a closer description of
the contents of the Gospel of Thomas and with the attempt to re-
construct the theology which it implies.

The Gospel of Thomas consists entirely of sayings attributed to
Jesus. There is no fixed formula of introduction. The normal cap-
tion is 'Jesus said'. 'The disciples' or 'his disciples' occur twelve
times, 'they said' or 'he said' (probably to be distinguished from
the disciples) five times. In two cases figures other than the disciples are introduced, a 'man' and 'a woman from the multitude', in
each case apparently drawn from the synoptic tradition.[1] Individual
figures either introduced in the course of sayings or as principal
figures in the context are Thomas, Simon Peter and Mariamme or
Mary twice, and Matthew, James the Just and Salome once each.
Probably for the sake of variety the dialogue form is introduced
on twenty-two occasions. In four cases alone is the introduction
more than very lightly sketched; and in all but one example a
synoptic background seems to be implied.[2]

The number of sayings is variously estimated by editors.
Doresse reckons 118, R. M. Grant 122, while the official translation anticipating the *editio princeps* enumerates 114.[3] The character of the Gospel naturally leaves a margin of doubt as to the
correct subdivision of the material which it contains. The sayings
are normally quite short. The longest occupies twenty-five lines
of the manuscript and only four others extend to more than fifteen
lines.

---

[1] Saying 72: Luke 12.13 f.; Saying 79: Luke 11.27 f.
[2] Saying 13: Mark 8.27–30 and parallels; Saying 22: Mark 10.13–15 and
parallels; Saying 100: Mark 12.13–17 and parallels. To Saying 60 no canonical
parallel can be found.
[3] Comparative table in Wilson, *Studies*, pp. 157 f. Gärtner accepts the
numeration of the official translation with marginal hestitation.

Many of the sayings resemble the canonical form of the teaching of Jesus, no doubt to give the maximum impression of authenticity. The important collection of parables is the special field of my collaborator, Canon Montefiore, and it is only necessary to point out the relatively large proportion of the material which it represents. Eleven sayings or portions of sayings are cast in the form of beatitudes, while two further sayings parallel the synoptic 'woes'. Gospel tags like 'He that hath ears to hear, let him hear' and 'many that are first shall be last' are introduced, though they are not confined to their synoptic contexts. Gärtner offers an outline sketch of the material from a form-critical point of view, using the classification of Bultmann, and calls special attention to the dialogue form[1]. If some examples occur in the later strands of the canonical tradition, it is clearly far more characteristic of gnostic documents. But the study of the literary forms of the sayings cannot by itself determine the vexed question of indebtedness to the canonical Gospels. If at times the resemblance is so close as to create at least a presumption in favour of this theory, the possibility that material independently transmitted should be cast in a similar mould obviously cannot be excluded. Still less can it be regarded as a decisive clue to the preservation of *agrapha*. Here the content of the material is even more important than its form.

It is difficult to discover any coherent principle of arrangement in the document as a whole. Whatever use the compiler may have made of written sources, whether canonical or apocryphal, they hardly seem to have provided him with the ground-plan of his document. Many sayings are related by catchwords such as 'light', 'bed', 'eye', 'children', 'rest', 'image' or 'persecution', though it cannot be assumed that in both cases the catchword chosen will be equally central to the theme of both sayings. Triple sequences also occur. Sayings 24–26 are connected by the themes 'darkness', 'the eye' and 'beam in the eye'. Sayings 47–49 refer to 'two masters', 'two in unity' and 'solitaries'. Sayings 63–65 form a group of parables, while sayings 99–101 are a set of variations on the theme 'I and mine' ('My Father', 'My brethren and my mother', 'Give me what is mine', 'Hating father and mother in my way'). One sequence of three sayings represents three variants of the theme of the fewness of the elect. The images of the harvester, the

[1] Gärtner, pp. 17–27.

well-digger and the bridegroom are successively laid under contribution to illustrate a single theme. Here we can see a saying in
the process of development. Saying 73 is closely related to canonical material. It is immediately followed by a saying independently
evidenced by Origen as from a gnostic source, 'Lord, there are
many round the cistern, but no one in the cistern.' The source may
be gnostic, but there are no special gnostic overtones. The third
saying, 'Many are standing at the door, but the solitaries are the
ones who will enter the bridal chamber,' offers a climax which is
more specifically gnostic in character. In one instance the arrangement is more complex and more subtle. The Preamble and the
first three sayings are united by a series of themes, 'the Living
Jesus' and 'sons of the Living Father,' 'the All' and 'the Kingdom',
'seeking, finding and knowing'. While in most cases there is no
reason to doubt that such connexions as can be traced were available in Greek, in at least one case the hand of a Coptic redactor
can be traced. The two halves of Saying 77 appear to be united by
a play upon words available only in Coptic, and the fact that the
second half of the saying occurs in a more natural context in the
Greek fragments from Oxyrhynchus virtually establishes the
point. Synoptic parallels to this method of compilation can be
found in the *Lesestücke* on the themes of 'salt' and 'light' in Matt. 5
and the sequence of parables in Matt. 13.

Yet if it is clear that the use of catchwords to determine the
order of material has been employed in the Gospel of Thomas, the
hypothesis cannot be plausibly extended to cover the document as
a whole. In one case (Sayings 56 and 111) there is an almost exact
duplicate. Two sayings, almost as widely separated in the collection as they could be, both depend closely upon Luke 17.20 f.[1]
Again, sayings with a similarity of theme do not appear to be
grouped together. Thus the question of religious observance is
the subject of Sayings 6, 14 and 104. Possibly their very separation
was intended to give them greater emphasis.[2]

An important feature of the Gospel of Thomas is to be found in
the questions asked by the disciples on such important topics as
Christology (Sayings 43 and 91), the Kingdom or the Kingdom of

[1] Sayings 3 and 113.

[2] R. Kasser (*L'Evangile selon Thomas*, Neuchâtel, 1961, pp. 155-7) gives a
useful table of catchwords and associated ideas partly in illustration of his
own theory.

Heaven (Sayings 20 and 113) and eschatology (Sayings 18, 24, 37 and 51). All these themes would have an obvious importance for the gnostic theologian. The question 'Whom are thy disciples like?' (Saying 21) would serve to introduce the theme of gnostic spirituality, while the question 'Who shall be great over us?' (Saying 12) has an obvious polemic reference against the claims of the Great Church. The subject of religious observance clearly had a bearing upon the domestic life of the gnostic communities as well as a critical side-glance at their catholic neighbours. Most are fundamental questions which gnosticism, in fact, shared with the Church, though the answers returned in or suggested by Thomas would hardly have satisfied a contemporary churchman. It is certainly curious that no question is asked about the status of the world and the place of the gnostic within or over against it, although the Gospel contains a good deal of material which bears on the subject. It is at least clear that the compiler did not use them as a framework for his collection. Thus we might have expected Saying 6 to attract Sayings 27 and 104. While Saying 51 is preceded by another saying which finds its climax in the concept of rest, other equally relevant material is to be found in Sayings 60 and 90 in the collection. No attempt is made to combine teaching on the Kingdom into a single block. It is, of course, possible that the dialogue form was introduced solely for the sake of variety and that the questions and answers were no more than a simple literary artifice, but it seems natural to describe them as the great questions seen from a gnostic point of view. The disciples' questions at least serve to give some indication of the leading themes of the work.

While certain principles of association (mainly verbal) can be traced between pairs or short sequences of sayings, no clear or orderly pattern emerges from the work as a whole. Yet it would be untrue to regard the Gospel of Thomas as a mere chaos of disparate material. Its unity consists not in the imposition of a compact and unified literary structure, but in a limited number of concepts or themes to which the compiler often returns in slightly different forms. The analogy of a set of themes with variations may not be too misleading provided that we do not expect one theme to be fully developed before another is introduced.

Any attempt to expound the theology of the Gospel of Thomas

must be preceded by a consideration of the character of the document and the purpose which it was intended to serve. Here certainties are few and we must proceed mainly by inference and conjecture. Whatever the character of its sources, it is clear that it was utilized and almost certainly compiled in gnostic circles. As we shall see, the Preamble and the opening sayings indicate that it was regarded as a gnosis. Its place in the Nag Hammadi collection puts the matter beyond reasonable doubt. An imposing list of parallels from gnostic and Manichaean documents is given in the commentaries of Doresse and Grant and employed with good effect in the exposition of Gärtner. Here, however, a degree of caution is advisable. Parallels from other documents certainly give an indication of the way in which the sayings might be used and can shed some light upon obscure phrases or cryptic ideas. It must not be forgotten that, as they stand, the sayings do not contain any explicit theological context. We look in vain for some of the more obvious gnostic themes and concepts. Aeons and syzygies are conspicuous by their absence, even in the relatively undeveloped form in which the former appear in the Gospel of Truth. The All occurs, but not the Pleroma. There is no explicit reference to the Demiurge, but there are a few indications that the idea was present in the compiler's mind. It is axiomatic that the sayings must have proved readily assimilable to gnostic purposes and in many cases a gnostic application lies close at hand. Yet if the gnostic systems may be just round the corner, they are seldom plainly in sight. No doubt top-heavy mythologies cannot be conveniently fitted into short logia, especially if (as seems probable) many of them were drawn from earlier sources with greater or less approximation to the canonical tradition. Into sayings of this type the full-scale gnostic systems would not completely go. The problem, however, remains of a document probably compiled and obviously used by gnostics, in which many of the distinctive gnostic ideas are either completely absent or left at the level of inference.

We can only move conjecturally towards a possible solution of this problem. While our knowledge of gnostic literature has rapidly increased during the last half-century, it is still impossible to give an adequate account either of the domestic organization or missionary apologetic of the gnostic sects. The serious nature of their impact upon the Great Church can safely be deduced from the nature of the counter-measures taken to meet the gnostic crisis. Evidently there was a significant competition for souls during the period. Whether R. M. Grant is correct in his conjecture that the initial impetus to gnosticism as we know it was derived from the disappointment of Jewish apocalyptic hopes, or whether (with Burkitt) we prefer to interpret it as an attempt to pass beyond early Christian eschatology to a more comprehensive world-view, there is no question that gnosticism might appear to provide (in Studdert-Kennedy's graphic phrase) 'food for the fed-up'. There may even be indications that the gnostics themselves had a careful eye for the possibility of conversions from the Great Church. The equivocal position of the 'psychics', half-way between the indubitably saved and the irretrievably damned, suggests an attempt to give some theological status on gnostic premises to members of the Great Church considered as a promising field for gnostic missionary propaganda. The *Letter of Ptolemaeus to Flora* not only gives a gnostic solution of the burning problem of the Old Testament, but also shows a gnostic propagandist handling a potential convert with great tact and considerable skill. There may even be traces of a process of 'reverse lease-lend' from the Church to gnosticism. This appears to be the most probable explanation of the use of sacraments in some at least of the gnostic systems. In view of the gnostic abhorrence of matter we should not have expected to find any trace of sacramentalism in their systems. If the acquisition of divine power for successful living was a widely felt need during the period, their interpretation of this power as communicated through saving mystical knowledge would appear to exclude its sacramental mediation. A probable motive for the acceptance of sacraments in some right-wing gnostic systems might be a realization that lack of them would be a severe handicap in the struggle for souls.

It is to this situation of spiritual competition and missionary propaganda that the Gospel of Thomas appears to belong. Polemical touches are not lacking. The position of James the Just, and particularly the promise to Thomas, embody the claim to possess an apostolic tradition superior to that of the Great Church. Indeed, Saying 13 rewrites the Confession at Caesarea Philippi to the detriment both of St Peter and St Matthew. The heritage of St Thomas in this saying is far greater than anything promised to St Peter in the canonical tradition. Whether the 'three words' represent a self-revelation of our Lord or (as appears more probable) a promise to St Thomas, the significance of the closing words of the saying is clear enough. Thomas is acclaimed as the master-adept, not merely the disciple who is as his Master but virtually the equal of his Master. The place of the women disciples in Thomas follows the general gnostic pattern and was almost certainly intended to serve the same end.[1] The accumulation of possible tradition lines may depend in part upon the sources of the Gospel of Thomas; it would hardly seem a disadvantage to those who used the document for apologetic purposes. The critical attitude to religious observance displayed in the sayings (though probably drawn from earlier sources) would be used in criticism of the worship of the Great Church, while the Pharisees and scribes who have received the keys of knowledge and hidden them could be applied readily enough to church leaders. Its inconsistency with the gnostic claim to possess an authentic tradition superior to that of the 'psychic' catholics might not appear too glaring to the gnostic propagandist.

Further light on the purpose of the Gospel of Thomas may be found in the concluding section of the *Letter of Ptolemaeus to Flora*, expressly addressed to a catholic inquirer. The question under discussion was a common problem; the status of the Old Testament and the manner in which it was discussed might not at first sight have come strangely to the Great Church. The concluding sentences which represent an invitation to inquire further and probe more deeply are significant for our purpose. 'For with God's help you will learn in order the beginning and the begetting of these (the aeons), if you are deemed worthy of knowing the apostolic tradition which we too have received from a succession together with the confirmation of all our words by the teaching of the Saviour.'[2] There is much here that might

[1] See an article on 'The References to Apostles in the Gospel of Thomas' written by my former pupil, Mr A. F. Walls, in *NTS* VII, 1961, pp. 266–70. I had already reached similar conclusions on the question of the 'three words'.

[2] Epiphanius, *Haer.* 33.7.9. An edition of the whole letter with full commentary by G. Quispel has appeared as *Sources chrétiennes* 24 (Paris, 1949).

be applicable to the Gospel of Thomas, though the parallel cannot, of course, be pressed to the point of identification.[1] We have already seen how St Thomas and St James the Just, as well probably as the women, could be built into a theory of apostolic tradition through succession, while a collection of sayings ascribed to the Living Jesus could form a powerful weapon in the gnostic armoury.

It therefore seems probable that the Gospel of Thomas was intended to serve as a kind of gnostic Testimony Book and, like other similar works, extant or inferred, it could serve a double purpose as a means of confirmation of the faith of the gnostic believer and as a stimulus to the potential inquirer. A convinced gnostic might derive considerable encouragement from 'the teaching of the Saviour', while the collection is also admirably adapted to the needs of the inquirer. An intriguing saying claimed as dominical, or a parable or saying sufficiently close to the canonical tradition to appear familiar and yet sufficiently different to invite further examination, might prove an effective instrument of gnostic propaganda. Indeed, one important saying, 50, reads like a piece of gnostic missionary briefing: 'Jesus said: If they say to you "From where have you originated?" say to them: "We have come from the Light, where the Light has originated through itself. . . ." If they say to you: "Who are you?" say: "We are his sons and the elect of the Living Father." If they ask you: "What is the sign of your Father in you?" say to them: "It is a movement and a rest." ' Beyond these conjectures we cannot at present advance with even a fair degree of probability.

An attempt must now be made to analyse the theological content of the document as a whole. It might at first sight appear impossible even to attempt to handle systematically so ill-ordered a collection of sayings, but, despite the apparent absence of any ground-plan for the work, the Gospel of Thomas gives a strong impression of unity of theme.

Here, however, a problem of methodology arises. All editors have called attention to a number of parallels to the sayings which occur in other gnostic and Manichaean writings. These are certainly significant and often close, but in the absence of closer

---

[1] Attention was first drawn to this passage by Grant, *VigChr* XIII, 1959, p. 173, and Wilson, *Studies*, pp. 12 f., independently of each other.

knowledge of the precise milieu of the Gospel it is genuinely arguable how far it is legitimate to adopt interpretations of particular sayings which depend too closely upon such parallels. For a parallel, however clear and significant it may appear, may itself be an interpretation of a saying or concept given in a particular gnostic school rather than the meaning originally intended by the author or compiler. The general problem of all exegesis, the extent to which the conclusions of the commentator are really contained within the passage itself, applies with peculiar force to a gnostic document like the Gospel of Thomas. It is partly a question of background and foreground and in the present state of the discussion it may be wiser to run the risk of under- rather than over-exegesis.[1]

The Preamble to the Gospel sets the stage for the subsequent sayings and gives the appropriate point of entry into the theological material. 'These are the secret words spoken by the Living Jesus and written by Didymus Judas Thomas.' Gnosticism cannot be accused of giving an insignificant place to Jesus, though there is much that is distinctive in its attitude to him. In common with other gnostic documents he is here described as the Living Jesus in a manner which goes beyond the accepted biblical usage. Normally in the Bible the title is applied to God, though, as Gärtner points out, the process of 'levelling out' or the transference to our Lord of titles normally applied to God, has already gone some distance within the New Testament itself.[2] The title recurs as a divine name in three logia (Sayings 37, 52 and 59), where it is not easy to say whether it refers to the Father or is transferred to our Lord. The Lucan question 'Why seek ye the living among the dead?' suggests that this description was particularly appropriate to the Risen Christ.[3] Within gnosticism it was a common practice to assign esoteric teaching to the Risen Lord, and to extend the Great Forty Days to eighteen months and even twelve years to give ample time for its transmission. While there is no explicit mention of any time factor in the Gospel, this remains almost certainly the context in which the sayings should be set. There is some evidence that the Christology implied in the

---

[1] See the cautious statements of Gärtner (pp. 92 f.).
[2] Gärtner, pp. 99–101.
[3] Luke 24.5.

saying follows the normal gnostic pattern. The relevant sayings here are 61 and 28. In the former, Salome appears to find a difficulty in the fact that our Lord had taken his place upon her bench and eaten at her table, and her doubts are only set at rest after Jesus has proclaimed his heavenly origin.[1] Saying 28 has been regarded as a possible *agraphon*, though Gärtner advances strong arguments against this conclusion.[2] The gnostic telltale lies in the opening phrase, 'I took my stand in the midst of the world and in flesh I appeared unto them.' A comparison of the opening phrase with Sayings 5, 52 and 91 suggests the description of the epiphany of a heavenly being, a veritable theophany, while the emphatic position of the words 'in flesh' (ἐν σαρχί) and the ὤφθην of the Greek version support this conclusion. While ὤφθη in the third person singular is fairly common in New Testament in this sense, the use of the first person singular is not a New Testament usage and would serve to reinforce the docetic implications of the whole phrase. Grant notes that the whole saying is strongly reminiscent of the description of the Revealer given in the *Hermetica*.[3] A further (though less direct) indication of the attitude of the Gospel of Thomas to the Incarnation may be derived from Saying 17, where a significant addition is made to a Pauline rhapsody put into the mouth of Jesus and probably related to his person and mission.[4] The gnostic gloss reads 'and which hand has not touched'. A comparison with I John 1.1 will serve to make the contrast plain.[5]

But the conclusion that the Christology implied in the Gospel of Thomas has a docetic ring may be supported by a further argument. While the solidarity of Jesus with the Father is a theme to which the sayings frequently return, there is a complete absence of any corresponding sense of his solidarity with ourselves.[6] While the restriction of the contents of Thomas to sayings and parables is obviously related to its purpose as a gnosis, it may be suspected that the compiler would have found the inclusion of incidents

---

[1] Gärtner, p. 132.
[2] J. Jeremias, *Unknown Sayings of Jesus*, ET, 1957, pp. 69–74; Wilson, *Studies*, pp. 41 f.; Gärtner, pp. 141–3.
[3] Grant/Freedman, p. 140.
[4] I Cor. 2.9.
[5] Gärtner, pp. 147–9.
[6] E.g. Sayings 15, 17, 19, 37, 52, 59, 61, 77, 83, 108.

derived from the earthly life of our Lord a positive embarrassment. Thus in Saying 100 the residuary traces of the canonical
saying on Tribute Money are purely minimal and the point
probably lies in a gnosticizing expansion of the original logion.
There is certainly an allusion to cross-bearing in Saying 55, but it
appears to be an unelided element in a synoptic saying applied to
the cost of gnostic discipleship. The Living Jesus does not carry
with him the marks of his passion. This is in sharp contrast with
the Gospel of Truth, which seems to come more realistically to
grips with the fact of the Passion.

In the Preamble the Living Jesus manifests himself as the
giver of gnosis. The 'secret words' are almost a technical term
for divine revelation. In other sayings the same theme is expressed
in different words. Thus Saying 62 combines the term 'mystery'
with a synoptically based saying which seems to imply that
authentic mysteries come from the right hand (the heavenly
realm) and not from the left hand (the place of the Demiurge).
The contrast between the hidden and the revealed is the subject
of five sayings.[1] But the disciples are as slow of heart to receive
the new teaching as they were in the canonical tradition to understand the teaching of their earthly Lord.[2] The Living Jesus must
therefore be regarded not only as the revealer but also as the
interpreter of the revelation which he brings. If this aspect is
more plainly expressed in other gnostic documents, it is certainly implied in the Gospel of Thomas and even hinted at in
Saying 1. The same saying proves that the teaching of Thomas is
regarded as a saving gnosis. 'Whoever finds the explanation of
these words will never taste of death' and the recurrence of this
phrase in Sayings 19 and 111 serves to confirm the view that this
gnosis is regarded as a life-giving mystery.

The knowledge which is its goal is interpreted mystically
rather than intellectually. Certainly there is an emphasis upon
self-knowledge which recalls at least formally the Γνῶθι σεαυτόν
of Greek philosophy, though the verbal parallelism must not be
pressed too hard. 'If you would know yourselves, then you will
be known', of which the converse is to be in poverty and to be
poverty (Saying 3). 'Whoever knows the All but fails to know

[1] Sayings 5, 6, 32, 33 and 108.
[2] Saying 92.

himself lacks everything' (Saying 67). Here is evidence for that 'passionate subjectivity' which Professor R. M. Grant finds so characteristic of gnosticism as a whole, though the contrast between self-knowledge and knowledge of the All does not support his view that the former is 'the chief gnosis of all'.[1] It seems as if two stages in gnostic spirituality are envisaged here, and this conclusion might be supported from Saying 2, which offers a sorites treatment of the gnostic *'ordo salutis'*. 'Seeking, finding and knowing' are arranged in a definite sequence, while the intermediate stages of 'being troubled' and 'wondering' appear to belong to the process of self-extrication from the human predicament. It is even possible that the relation between the two stages of knowledge presupposed in Saying 67 may be a kind of gnostic equivalent of the New Testament principle that faith without works is dead. Saying 3 refers to a knowing and being known of which at least the language would not have come strangely to St Paul.[2] To know or to reign over the All (Sayings 67 and 2), to find the Kingdom or to see the Father (Saying 27) and to be the sons of the Living Father (Sayings 3 and 50) are slightly different ways of expressing the goal of gnostic beatitude.

But what place in this chain of mystical experience was occupied by action? If the authentic New Testament combination of knowledge and action is conspicuous by its absence, this is not to imply that practical exhortations are completely lacking in the Gospel of Thomas. Thus Saying 6 contains a passage reminiscent of the Book of Tobit, 'Do not lie; and do not do what you hate, for all things are manifest before Heaven.'[3] The gnostic is exhorted to love his brother as the apple of his eye (Saying 25). Sayings 45 and 43 on trees and their fruit and the good and evil treasure, while no doubt patient of a mystical interpretation, are clearly reminiscent of the robustly ethical tradition of the Synoptic Gospels. While it might be superficially attractive to explain such passages as a mere matter of indebtedness to sources, the evidence is too strong to be convincingly dispersed by such methods. It would certainly be surprising if all gnostics were antinomians, and there is no reason to assume that moral earnest-

[1] R. M. Grant, *Gnosticism and Early Christianity*, 1959, pp. 8 f.
[2] I Cor. 13.12.
[3] Cf. Tobit 4.6 and 15.

ness was at a premium in the gnostic communities. Yet the impression that the Gospel of Thomas taken as a whole, while not neglecting ethical teaching, is vastly more concerned with a more mystical way is too strong to be ignored.

Gnosticism, then, as depicted in the Gospel of Thomas, is primarily a religion of salvation, though this is interpreted in a mystical and unbiblical way. The gnostic had an acute sense of the human predicament which he ascribed to man's involvement in the material world. In R. M. Grant's arresting colloquialism: 'For any gnostic the world is really hell.'[1] From this situation salvation by gnosis offered a way of escape which is usually conceived as a mystical self-extrication from materiality or as a release from the world and its contagion. With this is associated, whether as cause or (less probably) effect, a sharp-set theological dualism which is reflected in the Gospel of Thomas in a series of contrasts to which in slightly different forms the sayings in the collection return again and again.

The status of unenlightened man is depicted in a number of metaphors which are not in the main unbiblical except so far as their theological and spiritual context is concerned. He is in poverty and is poverty (Saying 3). Like his leaders (Saying 34), he is blind in heart, and empty and drunken into the bargain (Saying 28). He is dead, or at least in a moribund condition. Unless he looks at the Living One he will die and not be able to see (Saying 59). He is filled with darkness instead of light (Saying 61). He is in danger of being a corpse and being eaten (Saying 60), possibly a graphic description of impending personal dissolution. His very emptiness of soul will kill him (Saying 70).

This is no mere metaphorical statement of personal inevitabilities. For the gnostic, not only was the material world an environment inimical to the life of the spirit, but also the spiritual world itself was inhabited by hostile powers. To these there are a number of veiled allusions in Thomas. Gärtner's interpretation of the Samaritan carrying a lamb in Saying 60 remains at present no more than an attractive possibility, but there are clearer references in the strong man bound (Saying 35) and the thieves and robbers of Saying 21.[2] The parable of the *megistanos* who seems

[1] R. M. Grant, *op. cit.*, p. 150.
[2] Gärtner, pp. 166–9.

destined to be slain may also be intended to be understood in the same sense (Saying 98). A reference more neutral in tone may be found in the owner of the field to whom the little children surrender his field (Saying 21). The prospects of unregenerate man appear black indeed.

A wholly different prospect awaits the gnostics. They are described as the little ones or as little children, and as such will enter or know the Kingdom, behold the Living One and shall not fear (Sayings 21–22, 37 and 46). They are the elect of the Living Father (Sayings 23, 49 and 50). A special technical description of the gnostic is the 'standing one' (Sayings 16, 18 and 23). They shall not taste of death (Sayings 1, 18, 19, 85) nor see death or terror (Saying 111). They are men of light and have come from the Light (Sayings 24 and 50). They are filled with light (Saying 61). They are sons of the Living Father (Saying 3) and are taught to say to those who question them 'We are his Sons and we are the elect of the Living Father' (Saying 50). They will enter (Sayings 22, 113), know (Saying 46), see (Saying 113) or find the Kingdom (Sayings 27 and 49) and thus will reign over the All (Saying 2).

The contrast between the body and the soul, the flesh and the spirit, the dead and the living forms the theme of seven logia (Sayings 11, 29, 56, 60, 87 and 112). Here biblical warrant could certainly be found, though its dualism is never pressed too hard as in gnosticism and its thought background is very different. The Greek jingle σῆμα σῶμα indicates that it is not confined to biblical or gnostic sources. The importance of this theme to the compiler is established by the virtual repetition of a single logion, 'Whoever has known the world has found a corpse, and whoever has found a corpse, of him the world is not worthy' (Sayings 56 and 80). Here in the light of the similar variant in the Q Saying (Matt. 24.28; Luke 17.37) Gärtner is probably correct in finding the distinction between 'corpse' (πτῶμα) and 'body' (σῶμα) non-significant.[1] As it stands, the saying in either form is not free from difficulty. The closing phrase is obviously a word of commendation, and the meaning of the saying seems to depend upon some ambiguity of language. Does this lie in the word

---

[1] Gärtner, p. 160. See also the observations of K. H. Kuhn, *Muséon* LXXIII, 1960, pp. 318 f.

'found' meaning in the first half of the logion 'become involved in' and in the second 'found out' or 'detected'? Or is the word 'corpse' ambivalent, conveying its usual meaning in the first half and in the second paralleled by the curious Naassene usage of the term to describe the spiritual man? The note of scorn for the world, its intrinsic worthlessness and clogging materiality, is sounded clearly enough. The contrast between heaven and earth which will perish and pass away and those who live through the Living One is the subject of two further logia (Sayings 11 and 111).

A number of sayings combine the theme of the living and the dead with the metaphor of eating. We may begin with a phrase from Saying 11, of which we have already noted the opening phrase. The saying continues, 'In the days when you devoured the dead you made it alive'. There is no hint of a pejorative significance, and presumably it means that the dead things which the living eat become living themselves—a gnostic variant of the theme 'Whatever Miss T. eats turns into Miss T.' Similar language is found in Saying 60 significantly preceded by a logion which speaks of the living and the dead. It opens with an unexplained allusion to a Samaritan carrying a lamb on his way to Judaea. This is in itself sufficiently odd. It might lead us to expect a *reductio ad absurdum,* but in that case the whole saying seems to be suspended in thin air. Possibly it is intended to prepare us for a hostile action and to warn us that here eating must be taken in a pejorative sense. The absence of any known parallels to the basic incident makes interpretation extremely difficult. To our Lord's question 'Why does this man carry the lamb with him?' or more literally (with Gärtner) 'This person beside the lamb?' the disciples reply, with an apparent truism, 'In order that he may kill and eat it.'[1] Jesus virtually paraphrases their reply 'As long as it is alive he will not eat it, but only if he has killed it and it has become a corpse,' and points the moral 'You yourselves seek a place for yourselves in Repose, lest you become a corpse and be eaten.' Apparently this is a fate to be dreaded even by the gnostic disciple, and seems to express capitulation to the world and absorption into its materiality. On this interpretation the Samaritan would represent the world or some hostile power who

[1] Gärtner, p. 166.

is a foreigner to 'Judaea' and the lamb which he carries is the gnostic disciple, resident in a world in which he is spiritually a stranger. The world or its celestial patron wishes to kill him and will certainly succeed unless he finds salvation or a place of rest or (if the use of material drawn from the preceding saying is legitimate) life through the Living One. But much remains obscure, partly through the absence of any material which might throw light upon the incident and partly through textual difficulties in the passage itself. More puzzling still is Saying 7, which combines the theme of eating with a reference to a lion. Here the contrast between life and death (though it may be implicit) is not contained in the logion. It reads 'Blessed is the lion which the man eats and the lion will become man; and cursed is the man whom the lion eats and the lion will become man.' The difficulty here is that the lion seems to get the better of the bargain both ways and it is not surprising that suggestions for emendation have already been made. Presumably even gnostic scribes were not exempt from the dangers of homoioteleuton or similar causes of textual corruption. But what is the lion doing here and how is it to be interpreted? Professor R. M. Grant noted at an early stage of the discussion that lion's meat was believed in antiquity to possess medicinal properties, but it is difficult to see how this helps.[1] The possibility of a Christological reference to the lion of the tribe of Judah has also been noted, but this would at best cover half the saying. A more natural interpretation can be based on other gnostic documents and the Manichaean Psalm-book, and would explain the lion in terms either of the God of this world or as a symbol of physical desire.[2] In this case the contrast is between the gnostic who overcomes the world or his desires and the man who is overcome and absorbed by them, though even so the saying is obscurely expressed.

The contrast between light and darkness is, of course, biblical and recurs in the Qumran literature. It is not a gnostic invention, though easily adapted for gnostic use. The gnostic comes from the Light (Saying 50) and will return to the Light (Saying 11). He is the light-man or the man of light (Saying 24). As in the Fourth Gospel, Jesus himself is the Light that is above all

---

[1] Grant, *VigChr* XIII, 1959, p. 170; Doresse, p. 134.
[2] Gärtner, p. 163; Doresse, p. 134.

(Saying 77). Much here would be familiar to the writers of the New Testament, though it is set against a background which differs radically from that of biblical religion. The contrast between being filled with light and filled with darkness is the theme of Saying 61. The close connexion between the theme of light and the concept of the image is most clearly set out in Saying 50, where the gnostic is taught to say, 'We have come from the Light where the Light has originated through itself . . . it revealed itself in their image.' Further teaching on the subject of the images is given in Sayings 83 and 84 and is rather related to the gnostic theory of origins than with the basic contrasts with which we are concerned here.

Little need be said about the final form of the contrast, between riches and poverty. Saying 85 appears to compare Adam unfavourably with the gnostic, despite his heavenly origin, though the text is uncertain at the crucial point. The great power and great wealth from whom he came can only be God. By contrast unenlightened man who lacks even the lesser gnosis of self-knowledge is in poverty and is poverty (Saying 3). Yet with seeming inconsistency the synoptic beautitude of the poor is taken over almost unchanged. It can hardly refer to anyone other than the gnostic disciple.

One aspect of involvement in matter which the compiler held in special abhorrence is the fact of sex. Saying 37 is particularly striking. 'His disciples said: When wilt thou be revealed to us and when shall we see thee? Jesus said: When you take off your clothes and put them under your feet as the little children and tread on them, then shall you behold the Son of the Living One and you shall not fear.' This should be compared with the parable of the children in the field who restore it to its owner with a similar gesture (Saying 21). This is probably to be interpreted of the return of the world by the gnostic to its owner the Demiurge by self-renunciation. Whether this gesture is intended merely as a graphic simile or as a parabolic action must remain uncertain. The abhorrence of sex is clear on either showing. Two synoptic reminiscences seem to be drawn into this context.[1] Saying 37 is significantly preceded by a passage adapted from the Sermon on the Mount, 'Take no thought from morning until evening and

[1] Saying 36, Matt. 6.25 and 31; Luke 12.22 and 29; Saying 79, Luke 11.27 f.

from evening until morning for what you shall put on,' where the limitation of the synoptic passage to the question of clothes is probably deliberate and significant. Saying 79, which in its synoptic setting expresses the priority of discipleship over any human relationship whatever, is apparently intended to be read here in the light of the compiler's fastidious abhorrence of sex.

This portrait of man in his predicament depicted in terms of a series of sharply drawn contrasts was no doubt natural in what is essentially an illuminist type of religion. It posed, however, two questions, the one purely theological, the problem of origins, the second primarily spiritual, the problem of self-extrication. Both questions were in different ways decisive for gnosticism. Upon the determination of the first question depended its adequacy as a system of thought, while its answer to the second question represented its claim to provide lasting satisfaction for the spiritual needs of its contemporaries.

The problem of creation is frequently handled in the gnostic documents and forms a leading motif in the mythologies which they contain. There is, however, a sharp difference of treatment between the gnostic approach to creation and the attitude of the Great Church. In harmony with the biblical tradition as a whole, the Church regarded creation as a datum rather than a problem. Whatever the difficulties involved in such a view, its theologians claimed that the world was God's world and that creation was an activity in which it was wholly proper for God to engage. Admittedly something had gone wrong with the world, but this was a separate question, which the doctrine of the Fall was designed to answer. As it left God's hands creation itself was 'very good' and its subsequent fall was not an inevitable corollary of its existence. For the gnostic, on the other hand, the very existence of a material universe represented a problem of the first magnitude. The existence of spiritual beings (among whom the gnostics themselves were certainly to be included) raised no insuperable difficulties, although an agreed account of their nature and origin might be hard to achieve. But the plunging of the spiritual into the alien and hostile environment of matter proved much more intractable. It certainly could not be regarded as a datum for the gnostic doctrine of God. 'An enemy hath done this,' and the boundaries between the doctrines of creation and of the fall were

therefore swept away in order to give even a tolerable account of
the existence of the material universe.

The probable character of the Gospel of Thomas as an 'ice-
breaker' for potential converts, a document which might be used
as a preliminary to more detailed instruction in the gnostic
systems, or as the confirmation of these systems in the words of
the Saviour, supporting evidence of the Testimony Book kind,
naturally precluded any detailed treatment of these questions.
The utmost that may be claimed here is that Sayings 83–85 may
be derived from a gnostic exegesis of Gen. 1 and 2.[1] But this suggestion, while it has some attractive features, falls a good distance
short of demonstration. Daniélou has certainly called attention to
the importance of expositions of the early chapters of Genesis in
orthodox as well as gnostic thought.[2] References to 'image',
'likeness' and Adam occur in this group of sayings. On the
other hand, the obvious lack of unity of treatment in the sayings
suggests not so much extracts from a single document, but the
grouping together of themes (possibly from different sources)
ultimately derived from the Genesis narrative.

The Gospel of Thomas contains ample evidence for the importance of this problem in gnostic circles. In Saying 18 the question
of origins is brought into close connexion with eschatology. The
disciples ask our Lord, 'Tell us how our end will be,' but Jesus
diverts their attention to the even more difficult question of the
beginning. 'Have you then discovered the beginning so that you
enquire about the end?' The first question answered—and at
greater length than the other two—in Saying 50 reads 'From
whence have you originated?'

The origin of the gnostic himself does not raise in principle
any great difficulty. He comes from the Light where the Light
has originated through itself (Saying 50). The Light is clearly
self-caused and self-explanatory, and it is from this uncreated
Light that the gnostic springs. Two beatitudes contained in consecutive sayings bear on this question. The first occurs in Saying
18, 'Blessed is he who shall stand at the beginning, and he shall
know the end and he shall not taste death' where the quasi-
technical expressions 'stand' and 'not taste death' establish that

[1] Gärtner, p. 196.
[2] J. Daniélou, *La Théologie du Judéo-Christianisme*, pp. 121–9.

the gnostic is the subject of the beatitude. It is consistent with the idea of the pre-existence of the gnostic soul, though it gives no hint as to how this should be interpreted. The next saying opens with the words 'Blessed is he who was before he came into being.' The passage (or its probable source) is quoted both by St Irenaeus and Lactantius as a proof-text for the pre-existence of our Lord. Here, however, it is certainly applied to the gnostic believer. Further evidence for the origin of the gnostic may be found in another beatitude in Saying 49, significantly linked in subject with the opening question of the following saying. 'Blessed are the solitary and the elect, for you shall find the Kingdom; because you come from it, and shall return to it again.' Once again these are quasi-technical descriptions of the gnostic soul and, while its pre-existence may be implied, it is not certain whether this is conceived in personal terms or as an undifferentiated inclusion in the Light or the Kingdom. To this context also belongs the teaching about images in Sayings 22, 83, and 84, which are among the most difficult of the whole collection. Saying 83 seems to describe a hierarchy of three terms, the Father who is Light, the Image of the Light of the Father and the image revealed in the light-man or the inner light of the gnostic himself. The second term uses expressions remarkably similar to New Testament descriptions of our Lord himself, particularly in the Pauline Epistles, and may well refer to him. But the question of images is rather complicated than illuminated by the other two sayings. Saying 84 opens with a distinction between 'likeness' and 'image' which would not have come strangely to St Irenaeus. The former is not defined, but it may be that which distinguishes the gnostic from his unenlightened contemporary. The image is, however, further described. It came into existence before him and is undying, although it is not manifested at present. It is possible, as Gärtner suggests, that it represents a kind of guardian angel or celestial double of the gnostic.[1] The closing words of Saying 22, which speak of an exchange of images when the gnostic finally enters the Kingdom, may also refer to the replacement of the earthly image of the gnostic by its heavenly counterpart. But this remains at present an unverified hypothesis based upon the exegesis of cryptic sayings. It is clear, then, from the Gospel of

[1] Gärtner, pp. 205 f.

Thomas that the true gnostic comes from the Light and will return to the Light again. Language indicative of or reconcilable with the concept of pre-existence (though in no very precise sense) is used in this connexion. The document contains no clear allusion to the origin of the souls of non-gnostics comparable to the distinction between the 'hylics' and the 'psychics' of other gnostic writings.

But, whatever the difficulties involved in the origin of spiritual or potentially spiritual beings, they were as nothing compared to those raised by the existence of the material world. There are a few indications in the Gospel of Thomas of the existence of a Demiurge or of adverse powers more or less closely connected with the material universe, though in view of the general character of the document nothing very explicit could be expected. The problem is the subject of Saying 29, where it is virtually given up as insoluble. 'If the flesh has come into existence because of the spirit, it is a marvel; but if the spirit has come into existence because of the body it is a marvel of marvels. But I marvel at how this great wealth has made its home in this poverty.' Gärtner is probably right in seeing in the opening sentence two rejected alternatives, arranged in ascending order of improbability.[1] The language of the final phrase appears to be drawn from the Pauline description of the Incarnation in II Cor. 8.9, but the whole context appears to exclude this interpretation here. It may even be doubtful whether it is reconcilable with the gnostic interpretation of the Incarnation as the epiphany of a divine being, heavily weighted in the direction of docetism. The appeal to mystery at the crucial point could not be made more clear.

The second question which the gnostic was bound to face was how to extricate himself from this predicament. This was primarily a spiritual problem, though his particular approach to it had important theological consequences. Negatively world-renunciation was certainly involved. Thus Saying 27 opens with the words, 'If you do not fast from the world, you shall not find the Kingdom.' Gärtner recalls that the phrase 'fast to the world' was used in the early Church almost as a technical description of the monastic life.[2] What in the Great Church was regarded as the

[1] Gärtner, pp. 194 f.
[2] *Ibid.*, pp. 239 f.

special vocation of a relatively small minority was the standing condition of gnostic discipleship. The brief Saying 42 has been variously rendered, although its general significance is quite clear. The official translation offers 'Become passers-by', while Gärtner prefers the translation 'Become by passing away' with the meaning 'Enter into life by denying the world.'[1] One aspect of world-renunciation on which the Gospel of Thomas lays the greatest stress concerns the pursuit of riches, upon which it has little good to say. The long Parable of the Invited Guests who made excuses is given a more commercial setting than its synoptic counterpart, and its application is made plain in the concluding sentence, 'Tradesmen and merchants will not enter the places of my Father' (Saying 64). A Q passage relating to John the Baptist is taken out of its context and adapted to a similar purpose with the words 'Kings and great men are those who wear soft garments and they shall not be able to know the truth' (Saying 78). The Merchant seeking goodly pearls sells all his possessions to obtain the one pearl (the saving gnosis) (Saying 76). The gnostic is forbidden to lend at interest, though such action on the part of the man who ultimately discovers the Hid Treasure is not subjected to censure (Sayings 95 and 109). The discrepancy here may be due to the faulty redaction of original sources. Possibly the refusal of our Lord to act as arbiter in the matter of a disputed inheritance belongs to this group of sayings, though this fails to account for a significant alteration in the early part of the saying, and its principal point seems to relate to division within the family circle (Saying 72). Two sayings which are merely variants of a single theme call upon the rich and powerful to deny the world (Sayings 81 and 110). It is clear that the gnostic could appeal to the synoptic tradition for much of his material, though the dualist context in which it is set is alien to the spirit of the Gospel.

Eight sayings recall synoptic teaching on the cost of discipleship. Our Lord came not to bring peace but to cast division upon the earth (Saying 16). The refusal to divide an inheritance has an added tail-piece in which our Lord somewhat plaintively asks his disciples, 'I am not a divider, am I?', where an allusion to the division of families by the claims of discipleship is probably

[1] *Ibid.*, pp. 234 f.

indicated (Saying 72).[1] The synoptic demand to 'hate' father and mother is twice repeated in slightly different forms (Sayings 55 and 101), while our Lord's dissociation of himself from his family is recalled in two further logia (Sayings 79 and 99). It is impossible for a man to mount two horses, stretch two bows or serve two masters (Saying 47). Persecution is even foreshadowed in a pair of consecutive logia (Sayings 68 and 69).[2]

Faced by such radical demands, the gnostic resigned himself to belonging to a minority movement. saying 61 (in which this is the sole synoptic reminiscence) says bluntly, 'Two will be in one bed, the one will live, the other will die.' The same point is made in a saying already known before the discovery of the Gospel of Thomas, 'I shall choose you, one out of a thousand and two out of ten thousand' (Saying 23). Similar teaching is contained in a short sequence of sayings which open with an echo of the canonical tradition, though the final saying passes well beyond the limits of the teaching of the Great Church (Sayings 73–75). But the gnostic also took comfort from the fact that this elect minority represented a veritable *corps d'élite*, an aristocracy of souls. This is the point of a number of slight alterations made to synoptic parables. In the synoptic tradition the Parable of the Dragnet emphasizes the presence of good and bad fish within the total haul. It is, in fact, the classical proof-text for the Church as a *corpus permixtum*. In the Gospel of Thomas it has become the Parable of the Wise Fisherman who has selected the big fish from his catch (Saying 8). The Lost Sheep becomes the wether of the flock which is the object of the Shepherd's special care (Saying 107). The woman bakes large loaves from the Leaven (Saying 96), while in Saying 20 the mustard seed puts forth a large branch. The spiritual claims of the gnostic minority are not pitched particularly low in the Gospel of Thomas. In the important Saying 50 they are taught to say 'We are his sons and we are the elect of the Living Father', while the previous saying is a beatitude which reads, 'Blessed are the solitary and the elect, for you shall

[1] Another and less probable explanation which interprets 'divider' as 'heretic' is offered by D. Gershenson and G. Quispel in *VigChr* XII, 1958, pp. 19–26.

[2] On the basis of slight but insignificant alterations in the synoptic counterparts of these sayings, Gärtner (pp. 248 f.) interprets these sayings of the inner struggle of the gnostic.

find the Kingdom.' The paradox of the chosen few could not be more sharply expressed than in gnostic spirituality.

If the paradox of man's involvement in matter is expressed in the Gospel of Thomas by a series of sharp contrasts, we should expect to find that the process of mystical self-extrication leads to their annihilation. Here the crucial passage is Saying 22. The disciples have asked the question 'Shall we, then, being children, enter the Kingdom?' and our Lord replies, 'When you make the two one and when you make the inner as the outer and the above as the below, and when you make the male and the female into a single one so that the male will not be male and the female not the female, then you shall enter the Kingdom.' A further word must be said about some of these abolished contrasts.

(i) The outside and the inside. This contrast certainly has a counterpart in the synoptic tradition in the form of a Q passage from the Woes against the Pharisees.[1] Indeed, Saying 89 resembles the Lucan form very closely. The importance of this distinction to the Coptic editor is proved by a slight addition to Luke 17.21 in Saying 3, 'The Kingdom is within you and without you.' The final words are not found in the Greek version and can best be interpreted as an attempt by the editor to provide further domini-cal warrant for a favourite distinction.[2] In Saying 40, 'A vine was planted outside the Father which will be plucked up by the roots', the word 'outside' certainly has a pejorative significance. The addition in Saying 22 of 'above' and 'below' to 'outside' and 'inside' strongly suggests the cancellation of all four spatial dimensions in the interests of a new spiritual continuum.[3]

(ii) The male and the female. The annihilation of the distinction between male and female is the logical corollary of the gnostic repudiation of sex. Read in conjunction with the last saying in the collection which includes the startling words addressed to Mary (or Mariamme), 'See, I shall lead her, so that I will make her male,' it suggests a transposition of the female into the male. A similar notion is contained in other gnostic documents, one of which has been discovered in the present collection. Its appearance in

[1] Saying 89: Matt. 23.26; Luke 11.39 f.

[2] Gärtner, pp. 214 f., finds an allusion here to the dual existence of the Kingdom as both within the gnostic mystically and outside him in the heavenly world.

[3] A similar spiritual application is to be found in Eph. 3.18.

the last saying of the collection might suggest that it played an important part in the compiler's scheme of things, though too much ought not to be read into the sequence of sayings in a document seemingly as ill-ordered as the Gospel of Thomas. Even here a New Testament parallel to the language may be found in a passage from St Paul, 'There can be neither Jew nor Greek, bond, nor free, male nor female, for ye are all one in Christ Jesus.'[1] It is, however, a far cry indeed from a passage which speaks of the Christian Gospel as a reconciling force which crosses all human frontiers to the present saying which looks forward to the abolition of the basic distinctions of sex.

But whatever the cost of the gnostic's discipleship through world-renunciation, his primary aim was positive, salvation through gnosis. His pattern of spirituality was mystical throughout and it is possible to trace certain broad features of this mysticism in the Gospel of Thomas.

It is first and foremost an interior way. This can be seen most clearly in the interpretation of the Kingdom, a leading synoptic theme taken over and revalued in the Gospel of Thomas. The relative abundance of references to the Kingdom and the use of parables with strong resemblances to the synoptic might at first sight suggest that the similarities were greater than the differences. But even in the nomenclature of the Kingdom there is hardly a case in which it agrees exactly with the closest synoptic parallel. Possibly for reasons of gnostic theology the normal synoptic description 'The Kingdom of God' is carefully avoided. Preference is given to terms like 'The Kingdom' or 'The Kingdom of the Father', possibly, as Gärtner suggests, with the aim of accentuating the difference and (by implication) the superiority of the gnostic tradition.[2] While the synoptic expression 'enter the Kingdom' certainly occurs (Sayings 22, 99 and 114), other phrases like 'find' (Saying 49) and 'know' the Kingdom (Saying 46) which have no synoptic counterpart also occur. They are, however, wholly consistent with the gnostic interpretation of the Kingdom as an interior state of soul. This is supported by two significant logia which appeal to Luke 17.20 f. and where the much disputed ἐντὸς ὑμων is clearly interpreted as 'within you'

[1] Gal. 3.28.
[2] Gärtner, pp. 211–13.

and not as 'among you'. Saying 3 obviously has a polemic reference. 'If those who lead you say to you: "See, the Kingdom is in
heaven," then the birds of the heaven will precede you. If they
say to you: "It is in the sea," then the fishes will precede you.
But the Kingdom is within you and it is without you.' The saying
then concludes with a reference to knowledge and a contrast
between self-knowledge and poverty. Gärtner finds it impossible
to identify the false views to which the saying alludes.[1] It may,
however, be suggested that they contain a side-glance at the
synoptic description of the Kingdom as the Kingdom of heaven
and that the second view is a kind of parody of the implications
found in the first. In any case the rejection of the localization of the
Kingdom anywhere else than within man is clear enough. It is
'within you' and is closely connected in the compiler's mind with
the saving gnosis. In Saying 113 the disciples ask our Lord 'When
will the Kingdom come?'—a question which, as Gärtner points
out, is very similar to the eschatological speculations of the early
Church.[2] The reply, 'It will not come by expectation: they will
not say "See here", or "See there",' astutely quotes synoptic
material against the accepted doctrine of the Great Church. The
final conclusion, 'but the Kingdom of the Father is spread upon
the earth and men do not see it', interprets the Kingdom in terms
of gnostic interiority. A similar rejection of eschatology (without,
however, mentioning the Kingdom) occurs in Saying 51. The
disciples ask, 'When will the repose of the dead come about and
when will the new world come?' Jesus replies, 'What you expect
has come, but you know it not.' While the teaching of the
Gospels on the Kingdom contains both futurist and 'realized'
elements, the interior Kingdom of the gnostics could hardly be
other than realized.[3] It is perhaps surprising that the parables of
the Kingdom (though often subtly altered to fit the gnostic

[1] Gärtner, pp. 213 f.
[2] *Ibid.*, pp. 215 f.
[3] Gärtner is probably correct in interpreting the evidence as a complete
shift from the eschatological to the immanent. At the same time in Sayings 11
and 84 there are passages which refer to a crisis presumably still in the
future. 'When you come into the light, what will you do?' 'But when you
see your images which came into existence before you, which neither die nor
are manifested, how much will you bear?' This crisis may, of course, be
primarily mystical, but it may also be evidence that not even the gnostic
could completely ignore the eschatological perspective.

pattern) do not more markedly reflect this particular change of emphasis. Possibly this is an indication (whether consciously appreciated by the gnostic or not) that there was some material which they wished to include for other reasons which would not conveniently fit into this particular framework of reference.

The spirituality implied in the Gospel of Thomas is a type of unitive mysticism. The theme of unity runs through the document as a whole. In two sayings it replaces the synoptic 'faith' as the force which removes mountains (Sayings 48 and 106). The second saying has a more distinctively gnostic ring than the first. In other passages unity is the spiritual condition which results in the abrogation of existing distinctions. This is particularly clear in Saying 22: 'When you make the two one . . . then you shall enter the Kingdom.' The closing words of the next saying return to the same theme, 'They shall stand as a single one.' Saying 4 adds an additional climax to the synoptic echo 'for many who are first shall become last' with the words 'and they shall become a single one'. The reference throughout these sayings is probably to the healing by mystical attainment of the divided ontological condition of unenlightened humanity. There is an apparent exception to this teaching in Saying 11, a difficult and probably composite saying with an increasingly menacing undertone. It opens in a manner which bears some resemblance to the eschatological sayings of the synoptic tradition, 'This heaven shall pass away and the one above it will pass away,' and continues with the contrast between the living and the dead. The following phrase continues with a variant of the same theme and is introduced to the words 'in the days when' which serve as a link with the final clauses. The passage reads: 'In the days when you devoured the dead, you made it alive; when you come into the light, what will you do? On the day when you were one, you became two. But when you have become two, what will you do?' We should have expected the climax of the last phrase to be exactly the opposite. The normal gnostic *ordo salutis* would run as follows. Unenlightened man is divided. He realizes his condition, comes into the light. The dead become the living and enter a state of blessedness which can be described as unity. A possible explanation may be found in the theory that a composite saying has been constructed on the catchword principle without regard to unity of theme, but this seems to be little short of a counsel of despair. A comparison with Saying 84 (in which a formal similarity with Saying 11 has already been noted) leaves open another suggestion. Here (if Gärtner is on the right lines) the gnostic is depicted as already rejoicing in his 'likeness', but a day will come in some apparently future 'eschatological' situation in which he is confronted by his undying and pre-existent 'image'. This may be the situation described in Saying 11 as 'On the day when you were one, you became two'. In that case two incompatible conceptions of unity are contained within the Gospel of Thomas. Taken by itself either would be consonant with gnostic teaching, but they cannot be successfully combined into a single coherent whole. Neither view completely removes the difficulty.

A further aspect of gnostic spirituality is illustrated by a group of sayings upon 'solitaries'. The beatitude which opens Saying 49 reads: 'Blessed are the solitary and the elect, for you shall find the Kingdom.' It is the solitaries who will enter the bridal chamber (Saying 75). The gnostics who become disciples and accept the division of families which this entails 'will stand as solitaries' (Saying 16; cf. Saying 23, 'will stand as a single one'). The meaning of the word is not wholly clear. The Coptic merely transliterates the Greek μοναχός (monk) and it was thought at first that this might provide an indication of the date of the document. It is now, however, generally agreed among scholars that this is no more than a mere verbal association.[1] Even so it is not wholly clear whether it refers to a special class of advanced adepts among the gnostics or is a further description of the ordinary gnostic.[2] The scanty evidence could be interpreted in either sense, though in view of the idealized descriptions of the ordinary gnostic and the nature of the demands made upon him the second interpretation seems on the whole more probable.

---

[1] The suggestion was first made by J. Leipoldt in *TLZ* LXXXIII, 1958, and originally accepted by R. M. Grant in *VigChr* XIII, 1959, p. 170. Grant, however, withdrew his assent in an Addendum to his article on p. 179 in deference to the arguments of W. R. Schoedel.

[2] J. Doresse, p. 175, and W. Till in *BJRL* XLI, 1959, p. 452 n. 2, support the theory of a special class. Gärtner (p. 228) rejects it. The explanation of Grant and Freedman mentioned in the text of the chapter (p. 130) and favoured by Wilson may imply the theory of a special class, but this particular problem is not discussed in their commentary.

Grant and Freedman (quoted with approval by Wilson) explain the origin of the term as a reference to the breaking of family ties and therefore connected with the gnostic repudiation of sex. This is reasonable enough, but the promises made to the solitaries suggest a more positive connexion with the unitive way of gnostic spirituality. In the history of mysticism interiority and individualism are often found together.

It is not altogether surprising that this unitive way should be described in terms drawn from eating and drinking. Attention has already been directed to sayings which speak of the living as eating the dead and thereby endowing it with life. The metaphor is naturally ambivalent and a second application finds the point of the comparison in the destruction of that which is eaten. Both interpretations are found in the Gospel of Thomas. The clearest example of the first use occurs in Saying 11, 'in the days when you devoured the dead you made it alive', while the second application is probably the clue to the interpretation of the cryptic logion on the Samaritan and the lamb (Saying 60). The analogy of drinking again is capable of a double application. In Saying 24 it forms part of a description of unenlightened man, but a more favourable meaning occurs in Sayings 13 and 108. It represents the extension of the Johannine concept of the water of life to the conditions of gnostic spirituality. Thus in Saying 108 the promise is given, 'Whoever drinks from my mouth shall become as I am and I myself will become he, and the hidden things will be revealed to him.' This throws some much-needed light upon saying 13, where our Lord says to Thomas, 'I am not thy Master, for thou hast drunk, thou hast become drunk from the bubbling stream which I have measured out.' Here the context is clearly the *sobria ebrietas* of the mystical tradition and New Testament parallels have receded into the background. The adept is not merely like his Master; he has become his Master. The unitive way shows a persistent tendency to pass over into the conception of absorption into the Divine.

The last question which we are tempted to ask about gnostic spirituality—'What was its goal?'—is probably one which in this form at least would not have appeared meaningful to those who compiled or used the Gospel of Thomas. There is certainly some evidence which we shall need to assess for a measure of development in the spiritual life, a growth in mystical attainment, but this is balanced by other indications which give the impression of a fundamentally static character. This appears to be a permanent characteristic of unitive mysticism; gnosticism, it seems, does not provide an exception.

The evidence for some element of progress must first be briefly set out. There is first a group of sayings which are clearly indebted to the synoptic injunction 'Seek and ye shall find' (Matt. 7.7 f.; Luke 11.9 f.). Its very succinctness left ample room for development and its adaptation to a gnostic environment. In its simplest form this is provided by a straight addition to make its application clear (Saying 92). In Saying 2 seeking and finding are incorporated into a more complex pattern of spirituality. The suggestion of Gärtner that this betrays a sense of the inadequacy of the synoptic theme has much to commend it. The expansion has the object of intensifying the emphasis upon human effort.[1] The objects of this process are variously described, but suggest a fairly uniform picture of its goal. In Saying 38 it is Jesus himself, in Saying 60 it is a place of rest, and failure to find it means death. In Saying 24 the attention of the disciples is diverted from seeking the place where Jesus is to the contrast between light and darkness. Saying 76 speaks of the search for a treasure which fails not and which endures (the saving gnosis). In Saying 49 the disciples will find the Kingdom. Here are common themes, Jesus himself, Rest, the Kingdom, the treasure, light and life. The principle that attainment is through effort can be illustrated most simply by Saying 90. Here the promise of Jesus 'Come unto me . . . and I will give you rest . . . and ye shall find rest for your souls' is altered to 'ye shall find rest for yourselves' with the omission of the previous mention of rest as a gift. This need not appear wholly unexpected. It is not necessary to assume that all unitive mysticism is quietist.

There is apparently still room both for promises and warnings. The disciples shall enter, find or know the Kingdom (Sayings 22, 27, 46, 49, 99 and 114). They shall reign over the All (Saying 2). They shall live or not taste death (Sayings 4, 18, 19 and 111). They shall know that they are sons of the Living Father (Saying 3), behold the Son of the Living One (Saying 37), become as our

[1] Gärtner, p. 262.

Lord (Saying 108), see the Father (Saying 27). They shall stand as solitaries or enter the bridal chamber or the places of my Father (Sayings 16, 75 and 64). They shall know what is hidden, divine mysteries or the End (Sayings 5, 6, 17 and 18). They shall be filled or filled with light (Sayings 69b and 61). The list is impressive, but it is not easy to interpret as it stands. It is questionable whether these sayings are addressed to gnostics or non-gnostics or (more probably) to the former with half an eye on the latter. In some cases at least a general principle is put in the form of a promise in the future tense. It is even more important to observe that realities which are here put into the future are elsewhere described as present possessions. In the way in which our question is framed the gnostic might accuse us (in the words of another saying) of 'not knowing to test this moment' (Saying 91). Yet if the weight of the evidence can be reduced considerably by such methods, it still remains probable that some at least of the passages point to a goal of gnostic aspiration rather than merely to a present experience. As examples of warnings we may select three clauses introduced by 'lest', though an undertone of menace is not confined to these passages. Saying 21 includes the words 'lest the brigands (hostile powers) find a way to come to you'. Saying 59 ends with the phrase 'lest you die and seek to see him and be unable to see him', while Saying 60 has a similar conclusion 'lest you become a corpse and be eaten'. The caveats already entered with regard to promises also apply here with an additional difficulty. The gnostic knew himself to be one of the elect and could not therefore avoid the problem of indefectibility. Some types of gnostic at least seem to have regarded themselves as naturally and inevitably saved. Both with regard to promises and threats the absence of theological context for the sayings makes a decisive judgment difficult, if not impossible.

Yet the probability that the gnostic way of attainment did not exclude progress or even relapse does not seriously modify the impression that its character was fundamentally static. Its leading themes are interiorized and therefore already realized. There is an End and a Beginning, but there is no recognizable progress from the one to the other (Saying 18). The gnostic comes from the Kingdom and returns to it again (Saying 49), but it is already 'within you' (Saying 4). He has come from the Light (Saying 50), the light is in him (Saying 24), but a further stage of its self-manifestation seems to lie ahead (Saying 84). He is the son of the Living Father (Saying 3) and can live on the Living One (Saying 111), but is also heir to the promise that he shall not taste death (Sayings 1, 18 and 19). He will find rest for himself, but, like the new world, the rest of the dead is already here and is part of the sign of his Father in him (Sayings 90, 51 and 50). If there is some parallel to the eschatological tensions of the New Testament, it is to be noted that the framework which gives them meaning and cohesion in the New Testament is expressly excluded in the Gospel of Thomas. The spiritual situation to which the evidence which we have quoted appears to point is left without proper support. This general 'telescoping' of different aspects of a theme confirms the conclusion that the spirituality of our document is static in character.

This can be best illustrated by an exposition of two terms, the Place and the Rest (or Repose). In both cases the Coptic merely transliterates the Greek. Both are found in the New Testament, though usually in a general and non-technical sense. With one doubtful exception the wider meaning never occurs in the Gospel of Thomas.[1] The two terms are found together in Saying 60, 'You yourselves, find a place of rest for yourselves lest you become a corpse and be eaten', where the word corpse obviously has an unfavourable meaning. The most characteristic use of the word 'place' in the New Testament occurs in the Last Discourse in the Fourth Gospel, where it has an obviously eschatological reference.[2] The possibility of a similar background here is suggested by its association in two logia with the leading Johannine themes of Life and Light. Saying 4 speaks of 'the place of life', while in Saying 24 in response to a question of the disciples about the Place our Lord introduces teaching about Light. The form of the disciples' question plainly recalls the passage from the Last Discourse, while our Lord's reply (introduced by a solemn synoptic formula of emphasis) speaks of the man of light 'who lights the whole world', probably a reminiscence of the 'light that

[1] Saying 68, 'No place will be found there where you have been persecuted' (even here Gärtner, p. 249, detects a technical meaning), and Saying 86, where a synoptic saying has been expanded to bring the two terms together.
[2] John 14.3-5.

lighteth every man coming into the world' of the Johannine Prologue. The eschatological reference is, however, removed. Teaching about the Rest is, however, more complex. Its New Testament basis is clearly Matt. 11.28–30, which occurs in an abridged and amended form as Saying 90. We might have expected some use of Heb. 4, where the same idea (though not quite the same Greek word) summarizes the main theme of the chapter. The second theme in Hebrews, the Sabbath, is used in Saying 27, though it is clearly not derived from this passage. But it is probable that the author was not acquainted with the Epistle, whose canonicity was long in doubt even within the Great Church. Its immediate source in the Gospel of Thomas may well have been Jewish Christianity. Here Daniélou has recently pointed out that speculations based upon Gen. 1–2 played an important part.[1] Once again gnosticism turns what was originally an eschatological concept into a mystical term. Thus in Saying 51 the question of the disciples is thoroughly eschatological in form: 'When will the Rest of the dead come about and when will the new world come?' The reply of our Lord completely alters the context in which the term is set: 'What you expect has come about but you know it not.' The Rest which for the author of the Epistle to the Hebrews 'remaineth for the people of God' is a present possession for the gnostic who is the elect of the Living Father. The term provides the catchword by which this saying is linked to its predecessor. Here, in answer to the question 'Where is the sign of your Father in you?' the gnostic is taught to say, 'It is a movement and a rest.' This gives an unexpected turn to the whole idea. Movement and rest are set in sequence, if not also in balance. The introduction of 'movement' is hard to understand and is certainly not characteristic of the document as a whole. In view of the probable purpose of the logion as a preparation of gnostic missionaries the phrase might be a summary description of gnostic conversion and attainment. 'Movement' might cover the passage from darkness to light through world-renunciation, while Rest is a fairly obvious description of gnostic beatitude. Or it might describe successive stages of gnostic attainment along the lines of Saying 2. The probabilities are rather in favour of the first view. The comment of Grant and Freedman based on a

[1] Daniélou, *La Théologie de Judéo-Christianisme*, pp. 360–5.

passage from the Naassene source cited by Hippolytus, 'The movement is ultimately that of the unmoved mover', does not greatly help.[1] It is more likely to be a possible application of the passage than an indication of the intention of the author or compiler. On any showing a term unparalleled elsewhere in the collection cannot serve to inject a much-needed element of dynamism into the document as a whole.

Much of the material discussed in this chapter can be brought into better focus by a consideration of the concept of the All. A New Testament starting-point may be found in Col. 1.16 f. and 2.9, while a fair number of parallels are to be found in gnostic or gnosticizing writings. Gärtner finds a close relationship between the Gospel of Truth and the Gospel of Thomas at this point.[2] The importance of the theme to the Coptic redactor of our document is proved by two interesting alterations to the Greek version of the Oxyrhynchus sayings. The first occurs in the final clause of the sorites treatment of the gnostic way of salvation in Saying 2. In the Greek version the final clause is in a fragmentary condition, but comparison with a well attested *agraphon* suggests that it ran: 'He will reign and having reigned will rest.' There is a New Testament parallel to the word 'reign' or 'be a king' in a passage in the Pastoral Epistles.[3] The Coptic editor replaces the whole climax by the words 'he will reign over the All'. A careful reading of the Preamble and the first three sayings as a single unit strongly suggests that for the compiler the Kingdom, the All and the Living Jesus are virtually identical. The second alteration, a rearrangement of the Greek material, is equally significant. Saying 77 falls into two halves of which the first has no extant Greek parallel. This reads: 'Jesus said: I am the Light that is above them all. I am the All, the All came forth from me and the All attained to me.' This logion is not without difficulty. It apparently identifies Jesus, the Light and the All, and then proceeds to make some distinction between Jesus and the All. The All proceeds from him and attains to him. Here the parallel with the Gospel of Truth is particularly close, and reflects a distinctively gnostic combination of cosmology and

[1] Grant/Freedman, p. 152.
[2] Gärtner, pp. 145 f.
[3] II Tim. 2.11–13.

soteriology. The parallel between what is here said about Jesus and what is elsewhere predicated of the Father is so close as virtually to amount to identity. This is combined with one of the most attractive of the Oxyrhynchus sayings: 'Cleave a piece of wood, I am there; lift up the stone and you will find me there.' In the Greek version this is preceded by a form of Saying 30 which is a more natural introduction. The new combination of material in the Coptic text offers a more gnostic interpretation and establishes the sense in which the relationship between the Living Jesus and the All is to be understood. The All is also the subject of Saying 67. In its present form this is largely unintelligible, but it at least establishes that the All is the subject of gnosis. The whole group of sayings indicate a tendency in the Gospel of Thomas towards a mystical pantheism which (in the light of Saying 77) may fairly be described as 'panchristism'. Similar evidence is afforded by other logia, notably Saying 113: 'The Kingdom of the Father is spread upon the earth and men do not see it.' The unitive type of mysticism is particularly apt to result in pantheism.

This assessment of the theological content of the Gospel of Thomas is admittedly provisional, but it at least represents one way of building much of the material into some kind of unity. The nature of the document does not suggest that it was intended to embody a system of theology. A limited number of themes constantly recur expressed in different terms and without any recognizable unity of treatment. For this reason the spirituality of the Gospel of Thomas, which is at least relatively clear, has been selected as the most fruitful method of approach. Parallels in other gnostic documents are certainly of great importance as shedding some light upon obscure ideas or expressions. They may, however, be better evidence for the application of the sayings or similar material in particular systems than for the intention of the Gospel of Thomas itself.

There remains the problem of the relationship of the theology of the Gospel of Thomas understood in this sense to the teaching of the New Testament. It can be taken as certain that our document is based either directly or indirectly upon the New Testament, though it is probable that some extra-canonical sources were also laid under contribution. The four Gospels naturally take pride of place, but there are also a few fugitive echoes of the Pauline corpus. Even in some of the least promising sayings some tenuous connexion with the New Testament can usually be traced. But it is abundantly clear that the type of religion which the Gospel of Thomas presents differs radically from the New Testament stream in some essential respects. It may therefore be profitable in conclusion to draw out some of the main differences which seem to emerge. It cannot, however, be expected that an editor who probably drew on several sources should be completely successful in removing traces of doctrines and emphases which were foreign to his main purpose. Examples will be noted as they occur.

(*a*) We miss completely the tang of historical reality which belongs of right to New Testament religion. The place given to our Lord in the Gospel of Thomas is certainly no insignificant one. He is the Living One, the teacher and guide of gnostics, but he is not the Saviour active in history. Allowance must no doubt be made for the form of the Gospel, which confines itself to teaching and therefore lacks any full-scale narratives. The principle of selection is itself evidence of intention and gives no indication that the compiler assigned any real place to history in his economy of salvation.

This inference is supported by his treatment of the religious past. 'Adam came into existence from a great power and a great wealth and yet he did not become worthy of you. If he had been worthy, he would not have tasted death' (Saying 85). Solidarity in Adam was therefore meaningless for the gnostic. So far as he was concerned the prophets are dead and buried. 'Twenty-four prophets spoke in Israel and they all spoke about thee', to which our Lord replies, 'You have dismissed the Living One who is before you and have spoken about the dead' (Saying 52). The statement of the disciples (not here put in the form of a question) implies the Christological interpretation of the Old Testament, though the translation of its final words 'about thee' is not wholly certain. In the light of its emphatic rejection by our Lord it is hardly surprising that St Augustine, who quotes this saying without further notice of its source, attributed it to Marcionite circles. Its polemical intention is at least clear enough. The twenty-four prophets are either the twenty-four books of the Old

Testament as reckoned in the Talmud and the Mishnah or (less probably) the twenty-three prophetic books of the Old Testament (former, major and minor) with the addition of John the Baptist.[1] Other sayings which approximate more closely to the synoptic tradition are probably also to be understood in this sense. 'Whoever of you becomes as a child shall know the Kingdom and he shall become higher than John the Baptist' (Saying 46). Not without an eye to the Great Church, the Jews and their religious observances are swept away out of hand (Sayings 39, 43 and 102). Clearly the mystic way of the gnostics dealt hardly with the past. The future fares no better, and the eschatological perspective of the New Testament is virtually replaced by a felt interiority. The spirituality of the Gospel of Thomas is virtually static, and contrasts sharply with the dynamism of New Testament religion.

(*b*) Unlike the Gospel of Truth our document has no place for the Cross. Jesus is described as the Living One presumably with reference to his resurrection, but there is no allusion to the cross which to the gnostic appeared as an embarrassing and unreal preliminary. The suggestion of Doresse that the wood and stone of Saying 77 are veiled references to the cross and the stone laid at the mouth of the sepulcre deserves the brusque dismissal of Grant and Freedman.[2] Yet, inconsistently, the synoptic saying on the subject of cross-bearing is retained, presumably to enhance the demand for world-renunciation (Saying 55). There is no sense of sin. Those who come to our Lord and find rest for themselves are not described as the weary and heavy-laden (Saying 90). There is, it seems, a passage from death to life, but it has nothing to do with sin; it is the way of purgation from transience and materiality. Forgiveness only occurs in the mysterious synoptic saying on the subject of blasphemy against the Holy Spirit (Saying 44) possibly intended as a warning against rejecting gnostic teaching. This seems to be confirmed by the following saying in which the good fruit and the good treasure are to be understood as sound teaching.

(*c*) Again we miss the authentic note of the New Testament doctrine and experience of grace. The disciple is the mystical adept who 'finds Rest for himself' rather than the sinner saved by

---

[1] Gärtner, pp. 154 f.; Grant/Freedman, p. 153.
[2] Doresse, pp. 188 f.; Grant/Freedman, p. 168.

a downward movement of the grace of God. He is one of the elect, and hereby is introduced the fatal principle of the aristocracy of souls. The Parables of the Big Fish, the Large Loaves and the Favourite Sheep are significant here. It is a fundamental principle of New Testament religion that God has no favourites. Over against the gnostic aristocracy of souls is set the New Testament democracy of grace.

(*d*) We look in vain for any trace of the robust personalism of New Testament religion. Despite all the references to the Living Jesus, the Living One, the Living Father and sons of the Living Father, we are confronted in the Gospel of Thomas with a unitive and even an absorptive type of mysticism in which 'Whoever drinks from my mouth shall become as I am and I myself will become he, and the hidden things shall be revealed to him' (Saying 108). However close the terms in which the Bible speaks of the relationship between God and man, it never allows us for a single moment to blur the fundamental distinction between them even at the point of closest relationship. One of the greatest dangers of this type of spirituality is pantheism which results in 'a night in which all cows are black'. Of this the New Testament is refreshingly free.

It is therefore fair to conclude that despite the form in which it is cast and for all its impressive indebtedness to the canonical tradition, the thought climate of the document is alien to the world of the New Testament. As Professor R. M. Grant has put it, there is a warping, sometimes gentle, sometimes violent, in the process of transmission and compilation.[1] The Gospel of Thomas may have appeared to its compiler 'the secret words which Jesus the Living One spake'; despite the high claims of the rest of the Preamble they are not, for those who take the New Testament as their guide, the words of eternal life.

[1] Grant/Freedman, p. 108.

INDEXES

INDEX OF BIBLICAL REFERENCES

Bible Ref.	Page	Bible Ref.	Page
Mark—cont.		*Luke—cont.*	
7.16	64	11.9 f.	108
8.27–30	79	11.13	36
8.34	42	11.27 f.	35, 79, 95
9.48	36	11.33	57, 66, 68 f.
10.13–15	79	11.33 ff.	53
11.23	42	11.34 f.	53
12.1	49, 51, 54, 62	11.34–36	36
12.2, 4 f.	62	11.39 f.	102
12.8	63	11.52	35
12.9	77	12.3	36, 67
12.13–17	79	12.13 f.	38, 79
13.35	72	12.16–21	50, 57
13.35 f.	60	12.20	50
14.47	71	12.21	77
		12.22	18, 95
Luke		12.27	18
5.36	49, 65	12.29	95
5.36–38	64	12.33 f.	36
5.36–39	35	12.35	35, 72
5.39	65	12.37 f.	72
6.36 f.	35	12.39	35
6.39	35, 60	12.39 f.	42, 60
6.41 f.	51	12.40, 42 ff.	72
6.42	74	12.49, 51	42
6.43–45	34, 36	12.51–53	34
6.43 ff.	65	12.52 f.	51
6.44	53, 65	12.54 f.	73
6.45	66	12.56	36, 60, 74
6.45 f.	53	13.18	52
8.4	75	13.18 f.	51
8.8	48, 64	13.18–21	66
8.11–15	61	13.20	75
8.16	69	13.20 f.	50, 53
8.16 f.	53	13.30	60
8.19–21	34	14.7–24	74
8.21	60	14.16	61
9.23	42	14.16–24	61
9.58	75	14.17	58, 61
10.1–9	34–36	14.18	61
10.30	61	14.18–20	48

INDEX OF REFERENCES TO THE GOSPEL
OF THOMAS

The Saying numbers (see p. 12 n. 1) are followed in brackets by those of the plates and lines of the photographic edition (see p. 40 n. 1).

INDEX OF NAMES

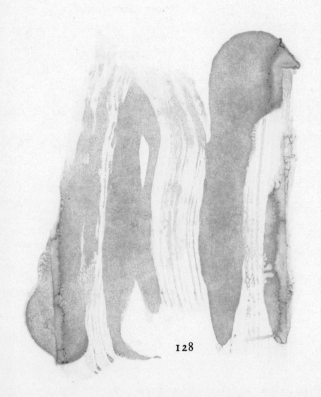